COMPLETE POEMS

Edith Södergran

Translated by
DAVID McDUFF

BLOODAXE BOOKS

ISBN: 978 0 906427 39 2

First published 1984 by
Bloodaxe Books Ltd,
Eastburn,
South Park,
Hexham,
Northumberland NE46 1BS.

www.bloodaxebooks.com
For further information about Bloodaxe titles
please visit our website and join our mailing list
or write to the above address for a catalogue.

Supported by
ARTS COUNCIL
ENGLAND

Typeset by Neil Astley at Tyneside Free Press Workshop, Newcastle upon Tyne.

Digital reprint of the 1984 Bloodaxe Books edition.

Edith Södergran

Contents

8	List of illustrations
9	Introduction
54	Poems/*Dikter* (1916)
84	Early poems from The Land That Is Not/*Landet som icke är*
94	The September Lyre/*Septemberlyran* (1918)
120	The Rose Altar/*Rosenaltaret* (1919)
144	Poems of 1919-20 from The Land That Is Not/*Landet som icke är*
148	Motley Observations/*Brokiga iakttagelser* (1919)
156	The Shadow of the Future/*Framtidens skugga* (1920)
178	Thoughts about Nature/*Tankar om naturen*
182	Last poems from The Land That Is Not/*Landet som icke är*
191	Index of titles and first lines

List of Illustrations

Frontispiece

1   Edith Södergran in the Raivola woods

Pages 13 to 16

2   Edith Södergran aged five
3 & 4 Two undated photographs of the young Edith
5   Edith Södergran, circa 1910-11

Pages 23 to 26

6   Edith Södergran with her cat Totti, 1917
7 & 8 Two more cat pictures from Edith Södergran's
     photograph album
9   Edith Södergran in the Raivola woods

Pages 39 to 42

10   The Södergran dacha at Raivola
11   View of Raivola showing the Russian church
12   Edith Södergran on her sickbed
13   Helena Holmroos Södergran
14   Henri Cottier, circa 1909
15   Matts Södergran
16   Cartoon of Hagar Olsson by Signe Hammarsten-Jansen
17   The sanatorium at Nummela in Finland
18   This photograph of Davos was probably taken by
     Edith Södergran

Introduction

Edith Södergran was born in 1892, and lived in Finland for most of her life. Finland has been traditionally subject to the influence of Sweden to the west, and of Russia to the east. The Swedes dominated Finland until 1808, and colonised its west coast. Thus a Swedish-speaking minority established itself in the country as peasants and fishermen, but also as administrative functionaries. Matts Södergran, Edith's father, came from this Swedish background, as did her mother, Helena Holmroos. Another circumstance saw to it that the family was influenced by the Russian presence to the east. Matts Södergran, an engineer who had travelled all over northern Europe, finally settled in St Petersburg. It was here that Edith was born.

A few months after the birth, Matts took his family away from St Petersburg during a cholera epidemic to a little village called Raivola, situated on the Karelian isthmus some sixty kilometres from St Petersburg, just behind the Finnish border. Raivola was a poor settlement which served in the summer as a villa resort for the intelligentsia of St Petersburg. It stood away from the sea, on the edge of one of the many Finnish lakes. The surrounding district had a distinctly Russian quality. Most of the villas were dachas in the Russian style, with brightly painted balconies, verandahs and windows. The church at Raivola was also Russian, with onion-shaped domes surrounded by birch trees and a Russian cemetery. Loup de Fages, in his critical study of Edith Södergran, writes of the place: 'Raivola had an unreal and fairytale atmosphere in its surrounding of forests and lakes. A population of sharp contrasts, as regards both material conditions and language. It was only after the revolution of 1917 that Raivola, from then on cut off from its Russian hinterland, lost near a burning frontier with its impoverished, even ruined population, acquired little by little that air of neglect, that atmosphere of romantic decadence which have struck the few visitors to the place, and which were to mark the poetry of Edith Södergran with such a strange hue.'*

The Södergran dacha at Raivola was built of wood, with a dozen or so rooms for the small family and a few servants. A

*Loup de Fages, *Edith Södergran* (Paris, 1970), p.16.

9

Russian craftsman, an old man called 'the hermit', lived in a little outhouse. The garden was a small park – *gården* – planted with firs and maples. One side of the park gave onto the Russian cemetery mentioned earlier. It was in this house that Edith Södergran was to pass the greater part of her life.

Accounts of Edith Södergran's early childhood vary, but the consensus seems to be that she was not particularly happy. Her father was a man of simple tastes, while her mother was attracted to books and literature. Marital quarrels were frequent, and Helena Holmroos was driven increasingly to escape from these in reading and in the company of her daughter. A very close relationship formed between mother and child, one which did not end until Edith's death. Describing the photograph (see page 13) of the young girl at the age of five, Professor Gunnar Tideström has drawn attention to 'the sensual mouth and especially the eyes, which have a peculiar intensity, an expression at once observant and absent-minded.'*

When Edith Södergran was ten years old she was sent to school in St Petersburg. Her school education lasted six years. In the holidays she would return to Raivola, where her father continued to work. The choice of school was significant: Edith Södergran was sent to a German school, Die deutsche Hauptschule zu Sankt-Petri. This was a "prestige" school: it had 1600 pupils and had its premises on Nevsky Prospekt. It was strongly cosmopolitan in character. Modern languages and literatures were very high on the list of priorities, and the pupils came from every part of Europe, although Germans and Russians tended to predominate. Lessons in all subjects were given, and ballet was taught by one of the dancing masters from the Russian Imperial Ballet. Visits to balls, concerts and theatres were frequent, and museum trips included excursions to the Hermitage. Lessons and conversations were in German.

By the age of fifteen Edith Södergran had received a broad education which was international in outlook. Her health at this time already gave some cause for anxiety—she was infected with typhoid for a brief spell, and also suffered a form of trachoma. One of her former schoolmates, Sally Räikkönen, has left this account of their first meeting:

> In fact, Edith was already twelve when I came to know her in the second form of the Petrischüle, when she was introduced to her schoolmates at the beginning of the school year; she was a pale

little girl, with a face enlivened by large, bright eyes. I also noticed that her blond hair was very long and thick. She was at first very intimidated, which the schoolmistress did not fail to notice; she tried to give her pupil courage by telling her that in her class there were other Finnish girls ready to greet her. When the hour was over, I went up to Edith and asked her, among other things, if she spoke Finnish, and I learned that at home she spoke Swedish. We talked together in German.

Some time later, Edith's mother paid a visit to my parents; she had come in order to take me to see Edith. In this way we crossed a bridge over the Neva and reached the district known as 'Vyborgski', quite a long way from the centre; we entered a wide street flanked mostly by wooden houses. In one of these lived the Södergran family with their only child, Edith. Edith's parents looked older than my own, an impression heightened by the pince-nez of Mrs Södergran and the long beard of Engineer Södergran. These childish observations nonetheless made me well disposed towards the pair. What struck me especially was that Mrs Södergran smoked. I saw that very often Edith's parents had visitors. The whole company would sit round a large table. A lit samovar occupied the place of honour on the table and spirals of tobacco smoke floated in the room. The discussions around this table were endless, or so it seemed to me. But Edith and I had permission to walk in the courtyard. It was a very big level courtyard with large trees growing here and there, which Edith climbed. Wooden buildings looked onto this courtyard, possibly warehouses, against which ladders were placed. It was thus easy to climb up onto the rooftops. Up there we used to sit and talk in perfect peace and quiet about her life at school, or we would see a cat in the courtyard and run after it in order to stroke it. Cats occupied a special place in Edith's childhood, and in her early youth. She had made an entire album of cat photographs: on the roof we would often admire these cat faces. †

As Loup de Fages points out, this letter illustrates very well how Edith Södergran liked to sit on rooftops in order to spy out the land, and also how intense was her passion for cats. This latter fascination lasted all her life.

Between January 1907 and the summer of 1909, when she was between 14 and 16 years of age, Edith Södergran wrote some 225 poems. Of these, about twenty are in Swedish; five are in French, and one is in Russian. All the rest, the great

*Gunnar Tideström, *Edith Södergran* (Stockholm, 1949), p.18.
† Quoted in Loup de Fages, pp.22-4.

majority that is, are in German. It is doubtful whether she had read anything at all in Swedish by this time. Her mother had always lived in a Russian milieu, and her father could hardly write, so it is not very likely that either parent could have helped the child to develop her knowledge of her mother tongue. Edith Södergran was educated in German, it was in German that she spoke to her schoolmates, and her favourite authors were Heine and Goethe. As Professor Tideström notes, the main portion of Edith Södergran's school poems bear the strong influence of Heine: 'Sometimes there occurs an allusion to or an echo from the poet whom she later loved most, Goethe, but his influence on the poems' style can in no way be measured with that of Heine. It is the verse forms of the latter she usually employs, mostly the single three- or four-footed four-liners with the odd lines unrhymed, the even ones rhymed. And here are the typical moods of Heine: *Liebeswonne* and *Liebesweh*, "der Hohn, die Sehnsucht und die tiefsten Schmerzen". Like Heine she uses on the one hand a slightly abstract poetic vocabulary—"süsse" and "zärtliche" "Liebchen" with red mouths and lily-white hands; "marmor-kaltes Herz", "Blümelein", "Sterne... am Himmelszelt", etc.—on the other hand nonchalant conversational terms and everyday words, easily rhymed—"obligiert", "ridicul", "kapriziöse wie eine Ziege", "Schnurrbart". But the alternation between these two word groups is naturally far less refined in the hands of the schoolgirl than it is in the hands of her master.'*

Poems in which the romantic world of knights and ladies, of frenzied horserides mingles with a curiously personal nostalgia are found beside poems which express a deep love of nature and an intense longing for a companion with whom to share this love. Numerous poems are addressed to Henri Cottier, a teacher of French at the Petrischule who seems to have held a strong attraction for the young schoolgirl. Olof Enckell has stressed that this teacher, who had the reputation of an 'anarchist' at the school, had a profound influence on Edith Södergran's intellectual development. †

The theme of death is ever present. Matts Södergran contracted tuberculosis in 1904. His daughter visited him in the sanatorium at Nummela in Finland, and was horrified by what she saw. In 1907 Matts died. The manner of his death

*Tideström, p.32.
† Olof Enckell, *Vaxdukshaftet: en studie i Edith Södergrans ungdomsdiktning* (Helsinki, 1961).

2 *Edith Södergran aged five*

3 and 4   *Two undated photographs of the young Edith*

5   *Edith Södergran, circa 1910-11*

filled Edith Södergran with a horror of sickness and disease.

One poem in particular, written on 22 September 1908, seems to characterise very well her sense of loneliness, of confusion about her place in space and time, and her longing for a companion, a 'heart' that will understand her and love her:

Ich weiss nicht, wem meine Lieder bringen,
Ich weiss nicht, in wessen Sprache schreiben,
Ich weiss nicht, zu wessen Herzen dringen,
Vor wessen Augen stehen bleiben.

Ich habe für mich selbst gesungen
Und bin schon müde geworden,
Was ist mir jetzt das verschneite Tal
Im kalten, weissen Norden,
Dort schluchzen die Fichten meine Qual.

Ich aber verfluche die Einsamkeit
Und suche in der weiten Welt
Nach einem Herzen
Und schau in der Menschen Augen.

Und suche eine menschliche Seele
Die mich verstehen könnte
Jedoch ihre Augen sind mir so fremd,
Sie schauen auf andere Dinge.

[I do not know to whom to bring my songs,
I do not know in whose language to write,
I do not know whose heart to move
Before whose eyes to stand.

I have sung for myself
And am already grown tired,
What is to me now the snowed-in valley
In the cold, white north,
There the pine trees sob my pain.

But I curse loneliness
And look in the wide world
For a heart
And look into people's eyes.

And seek a human soul
That could understand me
Yet their eyes are so foreign to me,
They look upon other things.]

17

As Tideström notes, this poem bears a certain similarity to one of Edith Södergran's best-known poems, written many years later, about the little princess who looks in vain for a heart and who finds the eyes of people so alien. Tideström writes: 'It is interesting also from another point of view. The first part has traditional form, in the second part the rhythm becomes broken and rhyme is abandoned. The change in the verse form is obviously connected with the fact that an emotion is breaking loose, an emotion which is so violent that it will not allow itself to be bound by a conventional rhythm, an emotion which gives grounds for the name of *Lebensangst*.' The line 'Ich weiss nicht, in wessen Sprache schreiben' is significant. From now on Edith Södergran was to stop writing in German. Apart from one poem in French, the poems which follow are exclusively in Swedish, the language which was after all her mother tongue. Tideström draws attention to the fact that her written knowledge of Swedish was inferior to her written knowledge of German. He notes that these early Swedish poems are artistically weaker than their German predecessors, and that they contain a number of linguistic errors, including spelling mistakes. 'Edith Södergran had at this time really read very little Swedish poetry, and both she and her mother had indeed grown up outside the boundaries of our language area. They spoke an archaically marginal and not entirely correct Swedish. Gunnar Ekelöf has recalled that Mrs Södergran even in everyday conversation used the plural form of verbs. And Edith Södergran, even in her mature poetry, was sometimes uncertain about word forms, gender, conjugational shifts, etc.'*

At the end of 1908 Edith Södergran contracted tuberculosis, probably as a result of infection from her father. A cure appeared to be possible and she was sent to the same sanatorium at Nummela where her father had died. The next five years were spent mostly in sanatoria, first at Nummela, then at Davos in Switzerland until 1914. The sanatorium at Nummela was the largest in Finland and even in Scandinavia. Loup de Fages describes it as 'a massive building, white and cold, in Germanic style, isolated in the woods at the edge of a lake which even to this day has retained a beauty that is wholly wild.' † Tideström gives an account, based on a diary impression, of how Edith Södergran looked at this time: 'She was small

*Tideström, pp.56-7.
† Loup de Fages, p.49.

built, slightly emaciated and comparatively small in stature. She looked tired and limp, she was pale and had "dark circles under her eyes". The limpness was only external, however. Her inner unrest and tension is witnessed to by a later jotting, which notes that she was *always* upset and nervous before medical examinations, which were rendered the more difficult by her irregular and shallow breathing.'*

The time in Nummela contained a crisis in Edith Södergran's life. 'Her external appearance was neglected. She was even "ugly, dirty, oily", says an observer, who at the same time stresses that there was an extraordinarily great difference between the young girl as she appeared during the time at Nummela and the worldly and elegant lady who later returned from Switzerland.' She concealed her terror of her illness under a habit of answering drolly and sharply to questions. In all, she presented a somewhat eccentric appearance, and there is reason to believe that her illness was then less physical than psychological: 'When the time came round for the doctors' visit, she had usually disappeared... She would be discovered on the roof of the kitchens...' Once she made a proposal of marriage to one of the male doctors at the establishment. Needless to say, this was refused. 'Some people took pity on the mother, who had no authority over her daughter, and sought to explain the peculiarities of the young girl by saying that she was spoilt and that she came from a Russian background. Others, including the female director of the establishment, saw in all this merely a mild derangement of the mind. To the patients who came into contact with her it was clear that they had to do with a person who was lively, original to the highest degree, but lacking in equilibrium, intelligent, mild, and yet coldly critical, now sarcastic or cuttingly ironic, now on the contrary gentle and benevolent, outwardly reserved yet burning inwardly.' †

She did not stay at Nummela all the time. Over a period of two and a half years she left and re-entered the sanatorium no less than five times. As soon as she felt the slightest bit better she would leave for Raivola. She dreamt of going to a women's college where she could pursue her studies of literature and philosophy. At Nummela she made extensive use of the library.

*Tideström, p.58.
† Tideström, pp.58-60.

In 1911 Edith Södergran refused to stay at Nummela any longer. She wanted to go to Switzerland, and in January 1912 she and her mother set off for Davos. The Davos of this time has been extensively described by Thomas Mann in his novel *The Magic Mountain*.* The hothouse atmosphere of sanatorium life, the stark contrast between material luxury and inner spiritual misery, the frantic search for pleasure in the face of death, the petty scandals and storms in teacups, the black flags, symbolising death, which hung from the windows of the sanatoria—all these need no further elaboration here. The Södergrans stayed at Hotel Meierhof, which is still standing, while Edith received medical attention at the sanatorium of Davos-Dorf.

At the sanatorium she was placed under the care of a man who was to become very important to her, Doctor Ludwig von Muralt. This former assistant of Eugen Bleuler had a keen interest in problems of psychiatry, although he had been compelled to relinquish his post with Bleuler owing to the activation of an old lung tuberculosis, and to seek the healthier climate of Davos, where he occupied the position of head doctor. At Davos he had become particularly interested in the psychological effects of tuberculosis. When Edith Södergran met him she was able to describe him in one of her English compositions for her teacher of English, an Australian lady called Miss Jenkins: '...something quiet and superior, charming and mild under a morose appearance... His hands have an expression of firmness and cleverness. His feet are perhaps a little long, but the sound of his steps is like exquisite music. His eyes are grey, but with a greenish sparkle, when he is smiling or amused. He speaks German with a Swiss accent, powerful and ingenuous.'

This was not the first time she had let her feelings centre on an older man, as the episode with Henri Cottier reminds us. And again there was no chance of it being a happy love affair. She felt inferior to Muralt, submitted to him, and thought of him as 'the impossible'. Her feelings can be observed in this

---

*There were several sanatoria in Davos, and Mann's wife Katia stayed at the large Waldsanatorium from March to September 1912. When writing *The Magic Mountain*, Mann drew upon Katia's highly descriptive letters, and did not himself visit Davos until January 1921.

fragment from another English "composition":

Today I had a great misfortune, which has broken my forces and my energy, so that every word and every step is an enormous effort to me. Never mind I write this composition. I will tell you my sad story of this morning... As I knocked at the door of the waiting-room, there came out the head of dr Muralt. Instead of inviting me a(nd) saying to me nearly this: 'Please, enter! Excuse me, that my arms are naked. Here is my darling between the pneumothoraxes and here is Professor Wilms from Heidelberg,' he looked at me furiously and said: 'Please, wait a moment.'*

At Davos, Edith Södergran began to discover English literature. In the library there she read Dickens and Swinburne, also the Border ballads and Shakespeare. She read Whitman, and the influence of his *Leaves of Grass* can be seen clearly in such poems as 'God' and 'Beauty'. She also began to learn Italian, and she read Dante, whose *Inferno* she sometimes pictured to herself as the sanatorium: 'empty conversation, chatter about death, illness, sleep, lying-cures and sitting.' Certainly the poem 'Hell' from *Dikter* (1916) concerns this Dantean vision of the sanatorium. But nature was ever-present as a backdrop to human life. Every day she could see from the windows of the sanatorium the green mountain meadows, the white peaks of the Alps and the dense forest.

In 1913 she made an excursion with her mother to Milan and Florence (the Mediterranean is the 'strange sea' in the poem of that name). On 31 May 1913 she was back in Finland. She was never to see Muralt again, but she did not forget him, and kept his photograph on her bedside table at Raivola until she died. † In 1914 war broke out, cutting her off from central and southern Europe, and coinciding with a sharp deterioration in her medical condition. The woman who returned from Davos was the one

who smiling and painted with rouge
threw dice for her luck
and saw that she lost.

The ring of the poem was the ring of her destiny, which she knew to be ineluctable. She had to go back once more to Nummela, which she loathed:

*Tideström, pp.63-7.
† Muralt is the 'tree in the forest' ('Trädet i skogen').

21

I wrote to the doctor an unreasonable and immoderate letter, but I hope that it will explain a few things to him. I have a dreadful and superstitious horror of Nummela. When I came to see my father, when he was ill, there, I experienced a fear without bounds, a dreadful horror of death, a fear of this illness, this slow conscious death. Here at Nummela I have never been able to escape from these horrible sensations; I have always felt myself oppressed there.*

Yet she was not wholly cut off from the outside world. In 1916 she managed to have her first book of poems accepted for publication, by Holger Schildt in Borgå. It is perhaps difficult to imagine now the unheard-of audacity, the shocking quality which was the principal impression made by these poems in the provincial literary atmosphere of Swedish Finland: poems which dispensed with rhyme, which drew their literary inspiration from Rimbaud and Whitman, and from expressionists like Mombert, Dauthendey and Else Lasker-Schüler—poets practically unknown in Finland at that time—met with blank incomprehension from the bulk of the press. 'Vierge moderne', 'Hell', and 'God' gave particular offence, and the wife of a country priest organised a petition among her friends which she sent to Schildt, asking him to issue a written certificate declaring that the poems were a forgery, not the work of their author. The reaction in Helsinki was better. Erik Grotenfelt wrote a sympathetic review in *Dagens Press*. But somehow the book was too advanced for its time and place, and a long time was to elapse before Edith Södergran's poems found a truly understanding audience.

The poems of *Dikter* (1916) display, besides the obvious originality and directness that were the real cause of the scandal they occasioned, a marked diversity of literary influences. Besides those already mentioned, there are clear signs of the influence of the Russian Bal'mont, and also of Edith Södergran's childhood reading of fairy-tales—Snow-White, the cat that spins the thread of luck, the maiden and the dragon. This fairy-tale element is of the utmost importance for an understanding of the Södergranian world. It underlies all the other themes of the poet's work and was the medium through which she sought to give meaning to her life and to the world in general. In 1917, when she was confined to bed as

* Quoted in Tideström, p.76.

22

6   *Edith Södergran with her cat Totti, 1917*

7 and 8 *Two more cat pictures from Edith Södergran's
photograph album*

9 OVER: *Edith Södergran in the Raivola woods*

the result of a severe attack of pulmonary bleeding, and wrote very little, she conceived the idea for an allegorical fairy-tale, ' the manuscript of which has been lost. This fairy-tale unfolded against a backdrop of islands: the island of the virgin, the island of midnight, the island of the hermit, and a lake which was never more beautiful than by the last ray of the November sun, a lake where the princess Hyacintha lived, surrounded by celestial beings.

It was at this time, too, that she learnt of the death of Ludwig von Muralt at Davos-Dorf. She let her imagination resuscitate the memories of Davos and Muralt, and experienced the bitterness of loss. She was 'vierge moderne'—neither a woman nor a man, a "neuter", nearer in spirit to a fact of nature, a material object.

In March 1917 the Russian Revolution broke out. Tension between the Russian and Finnish communities grew, and at Raivola there was the sense of being near to events of overwhelming magnitude and importance without actually being able to see anything very much of what was going on. Only a few clues were apparent: Raivola, being one of the first stations over the Finnish border, was a natural disembarkation point for political delegations; the Södergrans could hear the music of the military bands playing on the station platform. Excited beyond the bounds of patience, Edith persuaded her mother to accompany her on a visit to St Petersburg, now called Petrograd. By all the evidence, the journey must have been extremely long and exhausting, and on her return to Raivola Edith succumbed to another attack of bleeding. But something seemed to have stiffened her will to be active: she sensed the importance of the events that were taking place around her and wanted somehow to be a part of them. She believed that the Russian Revolution was a sign that the world was progressing to a new stage of its development. We know that at this time she was reading a great deal of Nietzsche, and she tended to interpret events in the light of his philosophy. There was nothing unusual in this, for one of her background and reading. The Russian symbolist poets Blok, Bely and Bal'mont shared this approach to reality, as did the Russian poets whom Edith Södergran admired even more: Severyanin, Mayakovsky and the futurists.

Although she realised that she could never hope to be popular with the broad public, Edith Södergran thought that she might be able to win over the elite of the literary world. In September 1917 she went to Helsinki and met as many Finland Swedish literary personalities as she could: Runar Schildt, Ruth Hedvall, Olaf Homén and Hjalmar Procope, Erik Grotenfelt and Jarl Hemmer, Hans Ruin, Eino Leino, Ture Janson, Alexis af Enehjelm, the sculptor Gunnar Finne, and others. Some of these people have written down their impressions of the strange young woman who had suddenly appeared in their midst. Jarl Hemmer, who together with Erik Grotenfelt entertained Edith Södergran to an evening of literary discussion at a restaurant, later described by her as 'one of the most beautiful memories of my life', has left an account of this meeting:

> I have never seen a being that was so identical with its poems. In her emaciated face and her enchanting gaze, a gaze that recalled moonlight on dark water, there was something mysterious and as if marked by fate. Her manner of speech was not like ours: between fits of coughing, paradoxes and ineptitudes shot forth as in some wild game of hide-and-seek; just when one felt she was approaching something like common sense, she would laugh and then proceed to turn the whole conversation on its head.*

Ture Janson writes:

> She was just as one imagined her to be, absolutely out of her element in the world, pale and unhealthy in appearance, but avid for conversation. †

The young critic Hans Ruin was summoned from his bed to meet the poet:

> It was about nine thirty when the doorbell rang once, briefly and discreetly. Kaisi and I were still in bed, since it was Sunday morning. I padded to the front door and asked through the locked door who it was who had rung the bell. The reply did not come at once, but I heard a voice say 'Edith Södergran'. Edith Södergran! I was well and truly dumb-founded. I asked 'Miss Södergran' to wait for a moment and I dressed as quickly as possible, though it seemed to take an age. When I opened the door I saw in front of me a lady in a brown muff, a fur around her neck and wearing a hat with light blue feathers. We greeted one another and I asked her to come in. She sank into one of the armchairs, put the muff under her chin and looked at me for a long time without saying a

*Quoted in Tideström, p.155.   † Quoted in Tideström, p.154.

word. At last she formulated a request: she would like my autograph. She took a leather-bound notebook from a small portfolio. I leafed through the notebook. There were several names there: Hjalmar Procopé, Runar Schildt, Erik Grotenfelt, etc. It was my critical notice of her poems that had provoked her visit. I asked her what she thought of my review. She replied: 'You must be a profound psychologist. No one has understood me as you have.' I became more curious and asked her if there was any one thing in particular that had especially caught her attention. 'Yes, when you say of me: the desire to think the impossible, to experience the fantastic is second nature to her.' She wanted me to write this sentence in her notebook. I thought she spoke in a curious fashion, uncouthly, with a pronounced accent. And during all this time she kept her muff to her face, almost under her eyes, and never stopped looking at me. She stayed for half an hour or so, but left suddenly, after I had said when speaking of human relationships that one should be careful when one gives time the opportunity of correcting the first favourable impression one has of someone. Without saying a word she got up, went to the door—I followed her without saying anything either—gave me her hand and—disappeared.*

Jarl Hemmer sums up Edith Södergran's visit to Helsinki like this:

She found us starchy, reserved, impersonal; only the bohemian Eino Leino corresponded fully to what she expected a poet to be. For she had a personality that was too extraordinary, too highly charged with her solitary exaltation for her contact with us to be even a little fruitful. Several times she interrupted the conversation with the strange question: 'Tell me, do you think I will be happy?'† Perhaps we did not understand quite what meaning the word 'happiness' had for this soul who thirsted only after the extraordinary, but we did not omit to stress that we believed in her future. She did not read a complete trust in our colourless faces—and as she had come to Helsinki alone, so it was that alone she arrived back at the villa with its luxuriant garden, never to return again.‡

Edith Södergran was now to stay in Raivola until her death. She spent the years 1917 and 1918 in an anxious and

*Quoted in Tideström, p.156.
† 'Lycklig': the Swedish word means "happy", but it also has overtones of "lucky", cf. German glücklich.
‡ Quoted in Tideström, p.155.

exultant contemplation of the revolution, and in the reading of Nietzsche. At nights it was possible to hear the sounds of the fighting and see the flash of the gunfire. Raivola lay very close to the garrison of Kronstadt, and was particularly vulnerable to the relentless process of division between Red and White that went on all through the civil war. Just inside a Red zone, Raivola was subject to attacks by White saboteurs, who cut the lines of supply from Petrograd and Helsinki. A famine set in. During these years the Södergrans, together with most of the rest of Raivola's inhabitants, came very close to starvation.

The poems of *Septemberlyran* [The September Lyre] represent the poet's reaction to the upheaval. Two poems, 'Prayer' and 'The World is Bathing in Blood' illustrate the ambiguous attitude she had to what was happening. The anxiety apparent in the first poem is in sharp contrast to the Nietzschean joy of the second. One April evening, Raivola was taken by the White forces. The childhood world of the garden and the pine trees seemed about to be torn to pieces by the violence of war. Edith Södergran felt her mental equilibrium slipping. A poem like 'The Whirlpool of Madness' shows this quite clearly:

Guard yourself – here you no longer matter – life and death are one before the frenetic joy of power...

There is a sense of panic at the unchained quality of events and the equally unchained state of the poet's psyche. There seems to be no restriction, no limit to the possibilities of destruction. The poet's character is a 'red rag' to a 'bull':

The bull has no horns;
he stands at the manger
and stubbornly chews his tough hay.
Unpunished the reddest rag flutters in the wind.

('The Bull')

The poems emanate a certainty that both the poet and the revolutionary forces are bent on destruction, on self-annihilation, 'so that God my live'. Mankind is on the road to a higher stage of development—the emergence of the superman, the man-god, entails the destruction of human beings, who must come to a realisation of their own weakness and nearness to death. Edith Södergran herself was acutely aware of her own impermanence. This is why she could neither align herself with her aristocratic past nor turn her back on it for the sake of a revolutionary future. Bengt Nerman has suggested that 'she chose a third way... She did not agree with anything. But she took precisely this as her starting-point: that she just barely managed to preserve her own nature, her own subjectivity. She laid herself open to her own contradictions, stepped from abstraction down to earth and let her experience take the form that was possible. This meant that in the moment of creation she drew a parallel between all things and was thus able to give birth to something entirely new in language... She sought her security not in a group or a class or a system, but in the total experience of meaning that only openness can give.' Nerman adds: 'I believe that Edith Södergran succeeded because she did not protest against death. She accepted it as a part of her life.'*

We may see the obvious influence of Mayakovsky and Severyanin in these poems, then, as a spur to increased vitality rather than a sign of inner kinship with these poets. Edith Södergran certainly wanted to 'épater le bourgeois'; but she saw this more as a spiritually quickening and curative mission rather than as a social or "anti-social" crusade. She was not on any particular side—she was on everyone's side, on the side of the world and on the side of God.

This acceptance of the whole vision, as opposed to the partial, opened her to her own childhood in a way that is not very common. As Loup de Fages points out,† her spontaneity would not allow her to use 'grands mots' when describing great events. In her poem on the death of Nietzsche, for example, Nietzsche is her 'father', the poet is a child kissing the cold stone of the grave:

> Strange father!
> Your children will not betray you,
> they are coming over the earth with the footsteps of gods,
> rubbing their eyes: where am I, then?

De Fages notes: 'This natural approach, which has remained entirely youthful, these extremely precise images of childhood spontaneously reaching the heart of adult problems,

*Bengt Nerman, *Människan som språk* (Stockholm, 1970), p.133.
† Loup de Fages, p.121.

this union of two poles that are normally opposed, are one of the most original—and one of the most marvellous—aspects of her poetic art.'*

The self-confident tone of the introduction which Edith Södergran found it necessary to affix to the published collection *Septemberlyran* perhaps betrays the anxiety she felt about their future reception by a literary press she already knew to be more or less lacking in understanding of her work:

> That my writing is poetry no one can deny, that it is verse I will not insist. I have attempted to bring certain refractory poems under one rhythm and have thereby discovered that I possess the power of the word and the image only under conditions of complete freedom, i.e. at the expense of the rhythm. My poems are to be taken as careless pencil sketches. As regards the content, I let my instinct build up what my intellect sees in expectation. My self-confidence depends on the fact that I have discovered my dimensions. It does not become me to make myself less than I am.

Her 'dimensions', needless to say, were the dimensions of the entire universe, which she had experienced as a personal crisis and which had led her to reject all partial positions. Such an experience seemed merely luidcrous to the critic of *Dagens Press*. On 4 January 1919, signing himself 'Pale Youth', he dismissed the poems of *Septemberlyran* as '31 laughing pills' and wrote a parody of the poem 'The Bull' called 'The Cow'. Referring to the passage in the Introduction about 'dimensions', he directed his readers' attention to the portrait of the poet which appeared in the publishers' Christmas catalogue and wrote that 'if the body fulfils what the face promises, the dimensions could be reduced by a couple of dozen ounces without harm to her poetry.' As Tideström points out, the reviewer could certainly had had no idea that he was writing about someone literally on the brink of starvation.

Other reviews were equally offensive. The poet was accused of megalomania and called a 'Nietzsche-crazed woman'. What had really drawn the ire and contempt of these critics was a notice Edith Södergran had published in *Dagens Press* before they had a chance to publish their reviews. Called

*Loup de Fages, p.122.

32

Individual Art, it had stated that the new book was 'not intended for the public, not even for the higher intellectual circles, but only for those few individuals who stand nearest the frontier of the future.' The poet could 'not help those who will not feel that it is the wild blood of the future that pulsates in these poems.'

> The inner fire is the most important thing that mankind possesses. The earth belongs to those who bear the highest music within them. I address myself to the exceptional individuals and exhort them to heighten their inner music, and build the future.
>
> I myself am sacrificing every atom of my strength for my great cause, I am living the life of a saint, I am immersing myself in the greatest that the human spirit has produced, I avoid all inferior influences. I look upon the old society as the mother-cell which must be sustained until individuals construct the new world. I exhort individuals to work only for immortality (a false expression), to make the highest possible out of themselves—to put themselves at the service of the future.

The notice ended with a plea:

> I hope I shall not remain alone with the greatness I have to bring.

It is easy to see how such a statement could have aroused the conservative critics. Totally caught up in her experience of oneness with nature, revolution and the cosmos, cut off from the everyday world of literary journalism by sickness and political events, Edith Södergran never even considered that her words might be construed as the ravings of a megalomaniac, a pompous and hysterical female aristocrat. Her insistence on 'the future' was seen as a craven alignment with Bolshevism, and her talk of 'height' and 'dimensions' as *folie de grandeur*. In order to overcome this tendency in an appreciation of Edith Sodergran's poetry—and it is a tendency that is not always entirely avoided even by her most devoted admirers (witness Tideström's constant reference to her 'disturbed' state of psychic health in his critical biography)— it is necessary to understand how complete was the experience that she had undergone and would continue to undergo until her death. She had absorbed the whole of the external crisis, both that of the outside world and that of her own ailing body, into a subjective pathos which every so often gave rise to the writing of poems. It is important to see that she regarded the willed and conscious development of this extreme subjectivity as a kind of duty, a holy sacrifice. This is what she means when she says that she is living the life of a saint. The victim of this sacrifice was her own body, and she tried to communicate the sacrificial act by means of another kind of sacrifice, more symbolic: the poem. Georges Bataille has defined poetry as a sacrifice in which words are the victims.* His contention is that poetry leads from the known to the unknown, and the images conveyed by the words it uses are doomed to disappear and die. Edith Södergran's poems are imagistic in the extreme—but the images (of childhood, of Raivola and the lake, the garden, and so on) are nearly aways used not for their own sake, but in order to render more vivid an ecstasy, a state of mind and soul. In a poem like 'Fragment', language is used to create a sensation of chaos, of time and space collided to induce a feeling of dizziness. Through her poems, Edith Södergran was trying to bring her readers into contact with the cosmic forces she had encountered. There is evidence that the act of writing the poems was for her a very arduous business. The excitement which accompanied their composition usually led to an attack of pulmonary bleeding. Thus the sacrifice was also a very real one.

Not all the reviews of *Septemberlyran* were as damning as the ones referred to above. Ragnar Ekelund sprang to the poet's defence, but his review was not published until 10 January. A literary feud began to develop around the book, until psychiatrists were even claiming in printed articles that the poet was either mad or immoral, or both, and a few literary "names" upheld her integrity and dissociated themselves from the published slanders. One review by a member of the latter group is of especial interest. Hagar Olsson, then a young Helsinki writer just beginning her literary career, wrote a sympathetic article about *Septemberlyran* in *Dagens Press* on 11 January. She wrote admiringly of the poems themselves, while deploring the damage their author had brought to her own cause by publishing accompanying 'explanations'. Quoting Nietzsche ('Der Autor hat den Mund

*Georges Bataille, 'L'expérience intérieure', in *Oeuvres completes* (Paris, 1971), V, p.156.

zu halten, wenn sein Werk den Mund auftut'*), Hagar Olsson reproached Edith Södergran for having set herself out on the market-place for the jeers of the crowd, and accused her of acting 'like some cheap chanteuse out to make propaganda for herself.'

This latter remark stung very deeply. A few days later Hagar Olsson received a long letter from Edith Södergran (whom she did not know personally) which began: 'You ascribe to me unjustly cheap motives for my public action.' She went on to explain why she had acted as she had done:

> I had asked for a selection. The publisher took a good part of the best poems out of the collection (thereby robbing the book of its weight).

She told the story of how the publisher had mutilated her work and how her publicity in *Dagens Press* had only been intended to forestall an attack which she knew already to be inevitable. Even so, one cannot help but feel that even had the book appeared exactly according to her wishes, the critical reception would hardly have been any the more favourable. The letter included some new poems which their author invited the critic to consider, and ended with a remarkable appeal:

> Nietzsche says: Ich ging zu allen, aber kam zu niemand. † Is it now to be that I am to come to someone? Could we reach a hand to one another? I am now launching my offensive against you, I want you to see me as I really am and I want you to show me who you are. Could there be a godlike relationship between us, so that all barriers between us would fall? I speak to you in a tentative, degrading language. Nietzsche is the only human being in whose presence I would be afraid to open my mouth. Are you the sea of fire I will plunge into? If you *laugh*, you are my own. If you do not laugh, you ought still to be worthy of the highest form of friendship, which Nietzsche advised his followers against on grounds of prudence.

Hagar Olsson's reply overwhelmed Edith Södergran. She believed that at last she had a found a companion with whom she could share the secrets of her experience. Hagar

---

*'The author must keep his mouth shut when his work opens its mouth.'
†'I went to everyone but came to no one.'

Olsson was her 'sister', to whom she could confide the most intimate secrets of her life. Edith Södergran's side of the correspondence between the two women was eventually published in book form, with a linking commentary by Hagar Olsson.* It makes painful reading. Involved in the hectic early stages of a career as a publicist and socialist literary critic, Hagar Olsson had little time to spare for her 'sister'. While the published letters give a valuable insight into the development of Edith Södergran's nature mysticism and her gradual movement towards the Sufism of Goethe and Rudolf Steiner, they also reveal how far the 'godlike relationship' fell short of the poet's hopes. Raivola was far from the Finnish capital, and in reply to Hagar Olsson's invitation to visit her there, Edith Södergran wrote:

> My charming young girl! Cannot come. Insomnia, tuberculosis, purse is empty (we live on the sale of our household effects and our furniture). What we have in Russian and Ukrainian securities could only be redeemed in the event of the fall of Bolshevism. If the insomnia gets better I will try to come in a few months, but no certainty of this. Now I have found what I need: your objective view, and you have brains enough for us both.
>
> May one ask: do you work for the cause in general, or will you meet certain individuals? Give a list of them, I want to capture certain souls. Hemmer to sing for the cause and Grotenfelt to sing or scrawl. Ragnar Ekelund does not come into my plans. I share *Severyanin*'s view that if a talent is a little boring it is not full enough of genius. Igor Severyanin is at present Russia's greatest poet. Saw him at a poetry reading, never spoke to him. But he is the one in whom I have a similar trust to the trust I have in you. *He is a very great power and should be ready for our ideas.* But we must first educate him, he has, to be sure, certain café-concert mannerisms and does not know how to discipline himself. He will be the bridge to Russia, with him we will certainly be able to get the best of Russia on its feet again. What do you think of Sweden? Will it go there? One fine day we will certainly seize hold of Europe. Do you talk directly to certain people and have you the intention of doing this? You must read the best poems of Severyanin, they would quicken and enliven you, even though he is submerged in the boudoir and you will not find our heights in him.
>
> I was reborn in September, whence *The September Lyre*. I knew suddenly with unmistakable certainty that a stronger hand had grasped my brush.

Ediths brev (Stockholm, 1955).

How old are you? Health? Nerves? I want you to be well and in full strength. Give a short biography! Mrs or Miss? Degree of education? Myself: residence: Raivola, Petrischülerin, tuberculosis from age 16, Nummela, Davos, pneumothorax, waiting for someone to invent a cure for TB.
We must be ruthless with one another and sharp as diamonds...
I have a sister and have not heard her wonderful voice. I want to see your inner being, what is holiest in you.

The style and tone of this letter, its peremptory demands for concrete action at an absolute level, demands it would be impossible to fulfil in "real life"—all this is typical of the letters sent to Hagar Olsson with great frequency by Edith Södergran, even though she often obtained no reply. Hagar Olsson found the memory of this unequal friendship so painful after Edith Södergran's death that it took her twenty-five years to bring herself to look the letters out and publish them. For those twenty-five years she tried to forget about Edith Sodergran and her own failure to meet the demands of a soul that had in many respects already crossed over into another world.

The 'Sister' poems of Edith Södergran's third book, *Rosenaltaret* [The Rose Altar], grouped under the heading 'Fantastique', illustrate the poet's violent attachment to Hagar Olsson, and her fear that her 'sister' would betray her:

My sister...
Has she betrayed me?
Does she bear a dagger at her breast – the light-footed one?
Answer me – laughing eyes.
('I Believe in My Sister')

The fear of betrayal was insistent. Edith Södergran had circulated a letter among the literary world of Helsinki in which she demanded that her friends should stand up and be counted: Hagar Olsson, Ragnar Ekelund, and others 'should take back their hasty condemnation of my press insertion' (the one about *Septemberlyran*). She based her demand on the authority of Nietzsche and claimed: 'I am an individual of an entirely new species. When I speak of the unheard-of [*det oerhörda*] in my art I am not talking of the content, but of the *species.*' This new insertion was hopelessly misunderstood. Most of the literary world in Helsinki considered it in the worst possible taste, and Hagar Olsson herself was by her own confession irritated at being solicited so directly for a reply.

She wrote a cross letter. Edith Södergran's answer was violent:

You have publicly exposed me to disgrace. I asked you if you thought that this insertion could be of *great benefit* to the cause. Naturally on the assumption *that you would reply* and *by no means in order to criticise you*. No one has ever acted like this towards me.

The worst of it for me is that I have lost the sister who had begun to play a wonderful role in my poetry. My health does not permit me to come to you. *If you can tear yourself away for 4 days I am now ready to receive you at any moment you please*. If you refuse to do refuse to do this, I wish to break with you *forever*, for I am *a person of irrevocable decision*.

... Remember that this letter is a letter of destiny. I will believe no letter—I demand a proof of your fair-mindedness in that you come here. With one whom I distrust I do not want to have any dealings and do not want to wait for her for several months. That is my character—I can be no other.

I demand that you pay the price of our friendship through this journey—otherwise I shall understand that I am to be alone. Bow before my will, Hagar, you are approaching something that more beautiful than any love, and we could experience that which is most wonderful.

And so Hagar Olsson published a long article in *Dagens Press* on 8 February 1919. She defended Edith Södergran against the attacks of the critics, and associated her with the "new wave" of poets and writers that was beginning to appear in the other Scandinavian countries. Of this defence Hagar Olsson wrote later: 'I wrote what my heart inspired me with at the time. I tried above all else to make people understand that an inspired poet like Edith Södergran spoke in the name of the spirit, of the god that lives in all our breasts, and not in the name of her private ego. And that all talk of self-assertion in connection with her was just as tasteless and stupid as it would be in connection with the great mystics who felt the presence of the Almighty in their own souls.'

At the same time, Hagar Olsson wrote to her friend saying she would accept the invitation to come to Raivola. Edith Södergran's reaction was one of joy:

Schwesterlein!
Welcome to Raivola. Will be at the station, from where it is 2 kilometres to our home. My mother is very pleased you are coming. The cat Nonno and the dog Martti will also greet you cordially, as will our *punikki* [household help] Aino.

10 *The Södergran dacha at Raivola*

11 *View of Raivola showing the Russian church*

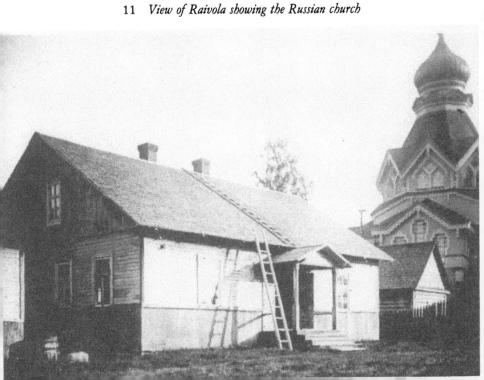

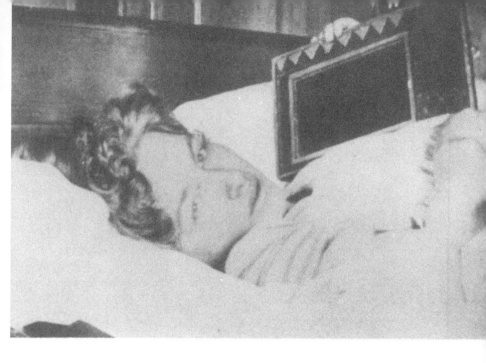

12 *Edith Södergran on her sickbed*

13 *Helena Holmroos Södergran*

14   LEFT: *Henri Cottier, circa 1909*
15   RIGHT: *Matts Södergran*

16   *Cartoon of Hagar Olsson by Signe Hammarsten-Jansson*

17   *The sanatorium at Nummela in Finland*

18   *This photograph of Davos was probably taken by Edith Södergran*

The night before your *malheur*-letter I dreamt that a beautiful black horse had broken loose at me. The night before the press insertion I dreamt that a herd of cows was following me with ringing bells and I also dreamt that I was walking along the street wearing a red cap and that a pedant of my acquaintance was nodding to me from the churchtower which you will see...

The visit lasted only a few days. Hagar Olsson has left a slightly vague account of it in her edition of Edith Södergran's letters to her. One has the sense that the meeting was an uneasy one, and that the temperamental differences between the two women were too great for there to be much real chance of any fruitful development of the relationship. Edith Södergran saw her 'sister' mainly as a vital link with the outside world, someone who was connected with the actualities of literature and politics and who could help further the 'cause'— the spiritual, moral and intellectual revolution of her dreams. But Hagar Olsson's preoccupations were more worldly, it seems, and in spite of her great admiration for Edith Södergran, her efforts to comply with the poet's wishes seem to have been largely in vain. Nevertheless, the two women continued to correspond, though it must again be stressed that the letters came mainly from Edith Södergran. Isolated in Raivola, stricken with an illness which she hated and saw as a deadly sin, a vice which had to be overcome, she had more than enough time in which to weave imaginary fantasies around her 'sister'.

That the friendship between the two was an unequal one can be seen from the many letters from Edith Södergran which begin *skriv* (write), *berätta* (tell), *titta* (look), and with ever-increasing frequency—*kom* (come). Hagar Olsson was engaged in journalistic work in Helsinki, and frequently travelled abroad as part of her activity—to Stockholm, for example, where she interviewed Ellen Key. Edith Södergran lived these travels vicariously and often made urgent requests for books— Nietzsche, for example, was unobtainable in Finland, but available in Sweden. Hagar Olsson tried to fulfil these requests as best she could, and tried to keep Edith Södergran informed of her activities. On one occasion she even went to visit Selma Lagerlöf, not so much out of personal inclination as because her friend wanted to know what the great novelist was like. But long spells would elapse between Hagar Olsson's letters, and throughout the correspondence Edith Södergran's complaints about this grow more and more frequent. In the meantime

Raivola was declared a restricted area by the Finnish military authorities, which meant that travel to and from it became extremely difficult. Nonetheless, Hagar Olsson did manage to make a second brief visit there in the summer of 1919, not without some early misgivings.

But how happy I was when I actually got out onto the country road, it was exactly as sun-warmed and happy and full of smiling delight as I remember all my summer roads to have been in Karelia. How well my soul felt in this nature, among these old Russian dachas, so inviting to the birds with their ornamentations and curlicues, which lay embedded in the luxuriant verdure and seemed to be mysteriously lost in their blossoming dilapidation. This was Edith's country, it should be seen in summer. She herself stood waiting outside her house, and I had the feeling that everything here was standing, waiting for something—the wonderful tall trees, the half-overgrown garden where a few yellow raspberries and bright red clusters of currants gleamed among the weeds, the warm den of the suntrap between the bushes of the courtyard, and the great abandoned dacha, the ghostly castle where no one could live any more and which was guarded by the enormous larch tree.* What was the old place waiting for, what was it dreaming about? It was so imbued with Edith's poetry that one involuntarily listened to its echoes when one walked in the garden under the catkins of the birch trees, and her own dreams about the future and the feast of two kindred souls seemed to wander around behind the locked doors of the empty, decaying house.

I stayed a little longer this time, and this was perhaps why I now had such a depressing insight into the truly Indian famine that reigned in the Södergran household. The situation had grown even worse. Even when she was able to procure a little flour, good Mrs Södergran was better versed in world literature than she was in the art of baking bread, baked, what is more, in an awkward old oven fired with home-gathered sticks and twigs, often green. It was dreadful to sit down at table. The food was such that it was hard to keep one's tears back when one thought that this was what a sick and utterly enfeebled human being had to live on. But at the same time a sense of tact forbade one to say anything that could have given offence or been badly received. The best thing that was obtainable was the milk, which they got on credit from the nearest neighbours, the

*This larch tree, which was taller than any of the other trees in the neighbourhood, appears in the poem 'I saw a tree...' (see page 54).

Galkins, but on no account would Edith drink this. These neighbours had an evil eye trained on her dear child, the beloved cat Totti or Råttikus, and one can understand therefore why the milk that came from them was 'evil' to her. Edith's mother appealed to me, and I did try to talk Edith round, but this was almost as heartrending as to see her leave her milk untouched, so real and deeply rooted in her emotions was her aversion to the Galkins' milk. For the first time I saw how completely it depends on psychological factors whether our food can nourish us or not.*

Between August and November of 1919, Edith Södergran wrote no letters to Hagar Olsson. The reasons for the silence are unknown, but it seems likely that during this time Edith Södergran experienced some kind of inner crisis, similar in intensity to the one she had experienced in the sanatorium at Nummela. The result of this new crisis was to be the collection of poems entitled *Framtidens Skugga* [The Shadow of the Future, 1920]. The last letter Edith Södergran wrote to her 'sister' before the silence reveals some of the elements of this crisis:

... Have all the time felt within me such an infernal *electricity* that it was almost too much to bear. As if I had lain in the arms of Eros himself the whole time. I feel like the most blessed creature of all that has arisen from the depths of existence. More than ever before it is now necessary to catch the mood. Have written poems, but this is not yet a period of inspiration. What I need is for someone to plunge a dagger into my breast. And there is no one I respect who can receive my suffering. Wound me, Hagar! If I could create now, everything I have written hitherto would be rubbish. This alone would be *me*...
... Near Christmas I shall publish a book called *Mysteries of the Flesh*... Schildt will gape, along with the rest of public opinion. It is Eros conducting worship in his own Temple. It is the same Eros who is the 'Wille zur Macht'...

The 'Mysteries of the Flesh' were the poems that later became known as *The Shadow of the Future*. The original title is more apt, and tells us more about the experiences that went into the poems. Until now, Edith Södergran's world outlook had been conditioned to a large extent by her extensive reading of Nietzsche. She had tried to persuade herself that

Ediths brev, pp.90-1.

45

she did not believe in God, that she was a materialist and anti-mystic. She saw her dreams vitalised in the image of the superman. During 1919, however, she had received visits from a retired schoolteacher, a certain Dagmar von Schanz, who lived near Raivola. Although Edith Södergran had no personal liking for this woman, it was through her that she became acquainted with the works of the anthroposophist Rudolf Steiner.* Steiner's nature mysticism seemed to her to form a direct link with that of Goethe. It also appeared to stand in resolute contradiction to the philosophy of Nietzsche. A severe conflict between the Nietzschean standpoint on the one hand and the Goethean-Steinerian on the other began to develop in the poet's psyche. It soon acquired the dimensions of a desperate struggle between apparently irreconcilable elements of her personality. With Nietzsche was associated the great accumulation of sensual and sexual energy that lay dammed up within her, denied release except through the medium of poetry. This is the 'Eros' of which she writes in her poems and letters. Steiner, and to a lesser extent Goethe, reflected her experience of childhood and nature, and ultimately of Christ and God. The poems of *The Shadow of the Future* show the conflict at its most acute, generating new forms of experience which carry Edith Södergran out of herself and into a transcendental mode of being.

The sense of intolerable restraint, of accumulated energy crying to be let loose, and threatening the human person, is the force that drives these poems:

> In order not to die I have to be the will to power.
> In order to avoid the atoms' struggle in their break-up.
> I am a chemical mass...
>
> ('Materialism')

There is an impression of enormous size, of enlarged dimensions:

> Eros does not see men's petty squabbles,
> he sees with his burning gaze
> how suns and moons complete their orbits.
> ('Eros is Creating the World Anew')

*It is perhaps relevant to note here that Steiner had a deep influence on other poets at this time, notably Andrey Bely in St Petersburg.

46

I lift up the riches of the earth on my shoulders.
                                      ('The Net')

In the light of blue heaven must the coffin stand blessed.
The coffin stands in eternity's room.
                            ('Resurrection Mystery')

Through my lips streams the heat of a god,
all my atoms are separate and on fire...
                                      ('Ecstasy')

This experience of immensity could be terrifying:

It is dangerous to desire when one is the powerful one,
therefore my desires stand still.
                                      ('Ecstasy')

Such statements inevitably brought accusations of megalo-
mania and even of madness from readers who thought that
Edith Södergran was talking about her own personal import-
ance and power. They overlooked a poem like 'Premonition',
for example, where it is clearly stated: 'I am only one among
others and others are stronger than I'.

The experience of increased size has nothing to do with any
sense of personal grandeur, but is rather the result of an
emotional charge, an electricity which filled her at this time of
crisis, rendering her normal perceptions invalid. There is even a
possibility that some of the poems may have been written
under the influence of a pain-relieving drug, although this has
not been proven. At any rate, the experience was a hallucinatory
one, though it was felt as intensely real, and was a way through
to an ecstatic vision of the kind described by Jakob Böhme or
Teresa de Avila. Certain late poems of Gunnar Ekelöf—in part-
icular, those of *Partitur* (1969)—bear a striking resemblance
to the poems of *The Shadow of the Future*. It is significant that
these, too, were written during a painful terminal illness.

In *The Shadow of the Future* there is a sense of giving-up, the
struggle for material existence is abandoned and the poet's soul
is freed. The victory is not achieved at once. Often there are
seemingly overwhelming doubts to be overcome. The soul
often seems unreal:

I do not believe in seeming and soul,
the game of games is so foreign to me.
                            ('Materialism')

Physical suffering intensifies her sensation of her own body's grossness and helplessness. Yet even this grossness and animality becomes transformed into a redeeming force, the power of Eros:

> My body is a mystery.
> So long as this fragile thing lives
> you shall feel its might.
> I will save the world.
> Therefore Eros' blood hurries to my lips,
> and Eros' gold into my tired locks.
>
> ('Instinct')

Throughout the poems there is a sense that at last her body is exhausted, that in some sense her 'I' is free of her physical self. Now that 'I' is at one with cosmic forces and dimensions, the human body, which has been the means towards this liberation, can fall back into passivity. Life is no longer "my" life, but the life of nature, of God. The transition to this standpoint must have been intensely painful for her, as she loved the perceptions of her senses and enjoyed in every way her presence on the earth. But as her illness progressed, she must have become aware that this indirect experience of nature was not for her. As her body grew weaker she began to experience herself for moments as a part of nature. Naturally her thoughts began to turn towards death:

> Truth, truth, do you lie in mortuaries among worms and dust?
> Truth, do you dwell there where is everything I hate?
>
> ('Hamlet')

She senses that she will not physically survive the onslaught of the forces which have been at war within her:

> My crown is too heavy for my strength.
> Look, I can lift it up with ease,
> but my remains will fall apart.
> My remains, my remains, you are wonderfully bound together.
> My remains, I believe you are beginning to long for a coffin.
> Now it is not the electric hour,
> my remains, you do not belong to me.
>
> ('Four Little Poems', II)

In the end, her body must count for nothing, her soul for everything:

48

But a little worm saw in a dark dream
that the moon's sickle cut his being into two parts:
the one was nothing,
the other was all things and God Himself.
                    ("There is no one who has time")

The story of Edith Södergran's involvement with Rudolf
Steiner need not concern us in detail. It is enough to say that
she was very well aware of the shortcomings of his philosophy,
inherent no less in his personality than in his books. But he did
bring her a measure of peace in the last, lonely years of her life,
and there can be no doubt that he was a catalyst, the 'dagger in
the breast' that made the writing of *The Shadow of the Future*
possible. There can also be little doubt that if ill-health had not
intervened, Edith Södergran would have certainly travelled to
Switzerland in order to become a pupil of Steiner. She
announced this several times in her correspondence with
Hagar Olsson. Such a discipleship would have been perfectly
in accord with Edith Södergran's dreams of establishing a new
world order of saints and mystics, poets and artists. Hagar
Olsson did in fact visit Steiner, partly out of a personal interest
and partly also to satisfy her friend's craving for at least some
second-hand knowledge of her idol.

Raivola was to remain, then, the place from which Edith
Södergran looked at the rest of the world. Raivola was the
'garden land' in which she wrote and suffered and meditated.
She was regarded as a curiosity by the other inhabitants of the
place. Residents have told of how she would sometimes be
seen standing alone in the courtyard of the dacha, staring up at
the sky to observe cloud formations. Sometimes the inquisitive-
ness of the neighbours turned to pure spite. In December 1919
Edith Södergran's favourite cat Totti, which meant as much to
her as a child, was shot by the Russian neighbours mentioned
earlier. An attack of Spanish influenza in early 1920 left her
weak and exhausted. All this time the civil war was raging.
Food was scarce, and Raivola seemed more cut off than ever
from the rest of the world. Desperately anxious to work, to be
of some use, Edith Södergran conceived the idea of preparing
a volume of German translations of Finland Swedish poetry.
Unfortunately the arrangement with the publisher fell through,
and the project came to nothing.

She did receive some visitors from the outside world during
the last years of her life. Elmer Diktonius, a literary lion of the

Helsinki avant-garde, came to Raivola and saw to it that she was able to write articles for *Ultra*, a literary journal of the new wave. But as a rule she was alone with her mother. More and more her thoughts began to centre on the person of Christ. Steiner and Nietzsche were forgotten. She read the New Testament. In 1921 the Kronstadt revolt erupted, and again the Södergrans could hear the shooting and see the flashes of gunfire in the night sky. The end came in 1923. Edith Södergran died while Hagar Olsson was on holiday in the south of France, where she received the sad news.

This was contained in a letter from Edith's mother, and a part of it read as follows:

> Do not think that Edith nurtured any bitterness towards Hagar because Hagar was not with her before her departure; she understood that Hagar was not travelling alone and perhaps had to comply with the wishes of her travelling companion. Certainly she yearned to see Hagar and on her last day she said: 'I wish Hagar and Diktonius were here.' And she was full of gratitude for all the proof of friendship she had received: she said the day before her departure: 'We have had so much help and friendship that I should write a book of gratitude, if only I could manage it.' And she often, often remembered all that Hagar and Diktonius had done for her.

The last poem Edith Södergran wrote contains these lines, which were engraved on her tombstone, now situated in the USSR at Raivola-Roshchino:

> See, here is eternity's shore,
> here the stream murmurs by,
> and death plays in the bushes
> his same monotonous melody.

Her destiny was to grow as one with her destiny—from her limited personal fate she aspired towards the condition of pure fate. Misunderstood in her lifetime—Gunnar Ekelöf described her as a Persian princess in Lapland—she became after her death one of the most widely appreciated poets of Scandinavia. Today her poetry is read and written about in all the Scandinavian countries, and her reputation there is comparable to that of Emily Brontë or Emily Dickinson in English-speaking countries, or to that of Anna Akhmatova in Russia. She has little in common with these poets. Her poetry, though imagistic in expression, is primarily a poetry of ideas. As such, it may remain alien to the majority of English-speaking readers. The present volume is an attempt to bring it to those readers, so that they may decide for themselves.

I gratefully acknowledge the support of the Finnish Literature Information Centre in Helsinki, which made a grant towards the translation of the poems. I should like to thank Thomas Warburton for his painstaking reading of the manuscript, and for his valuable suggestions. My thanks also go to Laus Strandby Nielsen, who many years ago introduced me to Edith Södergran's poetry, and to Neil Astley for his patience and perseverance in the editorial work on my translations.

The photographs come from the archives of Svenska Litteratursällskapet in Helsinki, who are shortly to publish a new book on Edith Södergran by Holger Lillqvist. I should like to thank Holger Lillqvist not only for supplying these photographs, but also for allowing us to publish several here which would otherwise have appeared in his book for the first time. The cartoon of Hagar Olsson was supplied by Museovirasto, the National Board of Antiquities and Historical Monuments in Helsinki.

The text I have followed in making my translations of Edith Södergran's poetry is essentially that of Gunnar Tideström's standard edition of 1949. I have, however, taken account of subsequent editions and reprintings (including the most recent) in which certain misprints and misreadings have been corrected. In the case of the posthumous *The Land That Is Not* (1925), I have followed Tideström's example in ordering the poems more or less chronologically, in their relation to what Edith Södergran actually published in her lifetime.

DAVID McDUFF

Poems (1916)

I saw a tree . . .

I saw a tree that was greater than all others
and hung full of cones out of reach;
I saw a tall church with open doors
and all who came out were pale and strong
and ready to die;
I saw a woman who smiling and rouged
threw dice for her luck
and saw she had lost.

A circle was drawn around these things
that no one crosses over.

The day cools . . .

I

The day cools towards evening . . .
Drink the warmth out of my hand,
my hand has the same blood as the springtime.
Take my hand, take my white arm,
take the longing of my narrow shoulders . . .
It would be strange to feel,
one single night, a night like this,
your heavy head against my breast.

II

You threw the red rose of your love
into my white lap –
I hold fast in my hot hands
your love's red rose that quickly fades . . .
O conqueror with cold eyes,
I take the crown you reach to me,
it bows my head down to my heart . . .

III

I saw my lord for the first time today,
trembling, I recognized him at once.
Now I already feel his heavy hand on my light arm . . .
Where is my ringing maiden's laughter,
my woman's freedom with high lifted head?
Now I already feel his tight grip around my shaking body,
now I hear reality's hard note
against my brittle, brittle dreams.

IV

You looked for a flower
and found a fruit.
You looked for a well
and found a sea.
You looked for a woman
and found a soul –
you are disappointed.

The Old House

How new eyes look upon old times
like strangers who have no heart . . .
I pine away to my old drains,
my gloomy greatness weeps out bitter tears
that no one sees.
I live on in the sweetness of old days
with strangers who build new dwellings
on blue hills up to the edge of the sky,
I talk softly with the captured trees
and comfort them sometimes.
How slowly time consumes the core of things,
and soundlessly treads fate's heavy heel.
I must wait here for gentle death
that will bring freedom to my soul.

Nocturne

Moonlit evening, silver clear
and the night's blue billows,
sparkling waves, numberless,
follow one another.
Shadows fall along the path,
on the shore the bushes softly weep,
black giants guard its silver in their keep.
Silence deep in summer's midst,
sleep and dream, –
the moon glides out across the sea
white tender gleam.

A Wish

Of all our sunny world
I wish only for a garden sofa
where a cat is sunning itself . . .
There I should sit
with a letter at my breast,
a single small letter.
That is what my dream looks like . . .

The Days of Autumn

The days of autumn are translucent
painted on the forest's golden ground . . .
The days of autumn smile at all the world.
It is so good to sleep without desire,
sated with flowers, of green grown tired,
the vine's red garland at the headboard of the bed . . .
The day of autumn has no longer any longing,
its fingers are so pitilessly cold,
in its dreams it glimpses everywhere
the white flakes' ceaseless falling.

You who never went out of your garden plot...

You who never went out of your garden plot,
did you never stand at the latticed view
and longingly watch how on dreaming paths
the evening toned into blue?

Was that not a foretaste of unwept tears
that burned like a fire on your tongue,
when over ways you never went
a blood-red sun went down?

I

I am a stranger in this land
that lies deep under the pressing sea,
the sun looks in with curling beams
and the air floats between my hands.
They told me that I was born in captivity –
here is no face that is known to me.
Am I a stone someone threw to the bottom?
Am I a fruit that was too heavy for its branch?
Here I lurk at the foot of the murmuring tree,
how will I get up the slippery stems?
Up there the tottering treetops meet,
there I will sit and spy out
the smoke from my homeland's chimneys . . .

A Strip of Sea

It is a strip of sea that glimmers grey
at the sky's end,
it has a dark blue wall
that looks like land,
it is there my longing rests
before it flies away home.

God

God is a resting bed, on which we lie outstretched in the
    universe
pure as angels, with saint-blue eyes replying to the greeting of
    the stars;
god is a pillow on which we lean our heads, god is a support for
    our feet;
god is a store of strength and a virgin darkness;
god is the immaculate soul of the unseen and the already
    decomposed body of that which has not yet been
    thought of;
god is the standing waters of the eternities;
god is the fertile seed of nothingness and a handful of ash
    from the worlds that have been burned down;
god is the myriads of the insects and the ecstasy of the roses;
god is an empty swing between nothing and all;
god is a prison for all free souls;
god is a harp for the hand of the most violent anger;
god is what longing can make come down to earth!

Violet dusks . . .

Violet dusks I bear within me from my origins,
naked maidens at play with galloping centaurs . . .
Yellow sunlit days with gaudy glances,
only sunbeams do true homage to a tender woman's body . . .
The man has not come, has never been, will never be . . .
The man is a false mirror that the sun's daughter angrily
    throws against the rock-face,
the man is a lie that white children do not understand,
the man is a rotten fruit that proud lips disdain.

Beautiful sisters, come high up on to the strongest rocks,
we are all warriors, heroines, horsewomen,
eyes of innocence, heavenly foreheads, rose masks,
heavy breakers and birds flown by,
we are the least expected and the deepest red,
stripes of tigers, taut strings, stars without vertigo.

Uneasy Dreams

Far from happiness I lie on an island in the sea and sleep.
The mists rise and fly and the winds change,
I dream uneasy dreams of war and great feasts
and that my beloved stands on a ship and sees
the swallows soar and feels no longing!
There is something heavy, immobile in his inner being,
he sees the ship glide into the unwilling future,
the sharp keel cut into refractory fate,
wings bear him into the land where all that he does is in vain,
into the land of empty and useless days far away from fate . . .

Vierge Moderne

I am no woman. I am a neuter.
I am a child, a page and a bold resolve,
I am a laughing stripe of a scarlet sun . . .
I am a net for all greedy fish,
I am a skoal to the glory of all women,
I am a step towards hazard and ruin,
I am a leap into freedom and self . . .
I am the whisper of blood in the ear of the man,
I am the soul's ague, the longing and refusal of the flesh,
I am an entrance sign to new paradises.
I am a flame, searching and brazen,
I am water, deep but daring up to the knee,
I am fire and water in free and loyal union . . .

The Colours' Longing

For my own paleness' sake I love red, blue and yellow,
the great whiteness is cheerless as the snowy twilight
when Snow-White's mother sat at the window and wished
      herself black and red as well.
The colours' longing is the blood's. If you thirst after beauty
you must close your eyes and look into your own heart.
Yet beauty fears the daylight and too many looks,
yet beauty will not suffer noise or all too many movements –
you must not bring your heart to your lips,
we should not disturb the noble rings of silence and solitude, –
what is greater to meet than an unsolved riddle with strange
      features?
A silent woman I shall be all my life long,
a talking woman is like the chattering beck that betrays itself;
a lonely tree on the plain I shall be,
the trees in the wood die of longing for storms,
I shall be healthy from top to toe with golden streaks in my
      blood,
I shall be pure and innocent as a flame with licking lips.

To All Four Winds

No bird strays here into my hidden corner,
no black swallow that brings longing,
no white gull that tides a storm . . .
In the shadow of the rocks my wildness stays awake,
ready to fly at the slightest whisper, at approaching steps . . .
Soundless and blue is my world, blessed . . .
I have a door to all four winds.
I have a golden door to the east – for love that never comes,
I have a door for day and another for sadness,
I have a door for death – that one is always open.

Our Sisters Walk in Motley Clothes

Our sisters walk in motley clothes,
our sisters stand by the water and sing,
our sisters sit on stones and wait,
they have water and air in their baskets
and call them flowers.
But I hurl my arms around a cross
and weep.
I was once as soft as a light green leaf
and I hung high up in the blue air,
then two sword-blades crossed in my inner being
and a victor led me to his lips.
His hardness was so gentle that I did not fall apart,
he fastened a shimmering star to my forehead
and left me shaking with tears
on an island that is called winter. –

The Last Flower of Autumn

I am the last flower of autumn.
I was rocked in summer's cradle,
I was put on watch against the north wind,
red flames burst out
on my white cheek.
I am the last flower of autumn.
I am the youngest seed of the dead spring,
it is so easy to die as the last:
I have seen the lake so fairy-like and blue,
I have heard the heart of the dead summer beat,
my chalice bears no other seed than death's.

I am the last flower of autumn.
I have seen the deep starry worlds of autumn,
I have watched the light from far-away warm hearths,
it is so easy to follow the same path,
I shall lock death's doors.
I am the last flower of autumn.

Pale Lake of Autumn

Pale lake of autumn
heavy dreams you dream
of a spring-white island
that sank in the sea.

Pale lake of autumn,
how your ripple hides,
how your mirror forgets
days that die.

Pale lake of autumn
it bears its high sky lightly and silently,
as life and death for one moment
in a drowsy wave kiss one another.

Black or White

The rivers run under the bridges,
the flowers glow by the roads,
the forests bow themselves murmuring to the fields.
For me nothing is high or low any more,
black or white,
since I have seen a white-clad woman
in my beloved's arms.

Autumn

The naked trees stand around your house
and let in sky and air without end,
the naked trees stride down to the shore
and mirror themselves in the water.
A child still plays in the grey smoke of autumn
and a girl walks with flowers in her hand
and near the sky's edge
silver-white birds fly up.

The Stars

When night comes
I stand on the stairway and listen,
the stars are swarming in the garden
and I am standing in the dark.
Listen, a star fell with a tinkle!
Do not go out on the grass with bare feet;
my garden is full of splinters.

Two Shore Poems

I

My life was as naked
as the grey rocks,
my life was as cold
as the white heights,
but my youth sat with hot cheeks
and exulted: the sun is coming!
And the sun came and naked I lay
all the long day on the grey rocks –
there came a cold breeze from the red sea:
the sun is going down!

II

Among grey stones
lies your white body and grieves
over the days that come and go.
The fairy-tales you heard as a child
sob in your heart.
Silence without echo,
solitude without mirror,
the air shows blue through every crevice.

In the Window Stands a Candle

In the window stands a candle,
that slowly burns
and says that someone is dead in there.
A few spruce trees stand silent
round a path that stops abruptly
in a cemetery in mist.
A bird pipes –
who is in there?

Wandering Clouds

Wandering clouds have fastened themselves to the
        mountain's edge,
for endless hours they stand in silence and wait:
if a chivvying wind wants to strew them over the plain
they should rise with the sun over the snow of the summits.
Wandering clouds have set themselves in the way of the sun,
the mourning pennants of everyday hang so heavily,
down in the valley life walks with dragging feet,
the sounds of a grand piano sing from open windows.
Strip upon strip is the valley's motley carpet,
firm as sugar is the heights' eternal snow . . .
The winter steps softly down into the valley.
The giants smile.

The Forest Lake

I was alone on a sunny shore
by the forest's pale blue lake,
in the sky floated a single cloud
and on the water a single island.
Ripe summer's sweetness dripped
in pearls from every tree
and into my opened heart
a little drop ran down.

The Starry Night

Needless suffering,
needless waiting,
the world is empty as your laughter.
The stars are falling –
cold and magnificent night.
Love smiles in its sleep,
love dreams of eternity . . .
Needless fear, needless pain,
the world is less than nothing,
from love's hand down into the depths
slips eternity's ring.

Words

Warm words, fine words, deep words . . .
They are like the scent of a flower in the night
that one cannot see.
Behind them lurks empty space . . .
Perhaps they are the curling smoke
from the warm hearth of love?

The Road to Happiness

We are not supposed to know
how miracles happen, –
there is no road to happiness,
no happy one can recall the path
that led him to happiness's secret door.

Alas, to hunt the bird of happiness
is to go without roads
and to take without hands.
To be king in happiness's fairy-tale
is to stand dumbfounded and amazed.

We wait for miracles from the day,
the day fades cold and pale.
Ask again, tired brain,
is your deam, the star of your happiness,
fraud and guile?

Forest Darkness

In the melancholy forest
dwells a sick god.
In the dark forest the flowers are so pale
and the birds so shy.
Why is the wind full of warning whispers
and the road dark with dismal forebodings?
In the shadow lies the sick god
dreaming venomous dreams . . .

In the great forests . . .

In the great forests I lost my way,
I sought the fairy-tales my childhood heard.

In the high mountains I lost my way,
I sought the dream-castle my girlhood built.

In my beloved's garden I did not lose my way,
there sat the happy cuckoo, my longing followed.

Luck Cat

I have a luck cat in my arms,
it spins threads of luck.
Luck cat, luck cat,
make for me three things:
make for me a golden ring,
to tell me that I am lucky;
make for me a mirror
to tell me that I am beautiful;
make for me a fan
to waft away my cumbersome thoughts.
Luck cat, luck cat,
spin for me some news of my future!

The Wood's Light Daughter

Was it not yesterday
that the wood's light daughter celebrated her wedding
and everyone was happy?
She was the weightless bird and the fair spring-head,
she was the secret road and the laughing bush,
she was the drunken and fearless summer night.
She was shameless and laughed without measure,
for she was the wood's light daughter;
she had borrowed the cuckoo's instrument
and wandered playing from lake to lake.
When the wood's light daughter celebrated her wedding
there was no one unhappy on earth:
the wood's light daughter is free from longing,
she is blond-haired and stills all dreams
she is pale and wakens all desires.
When the wood's light daughter celebrated her wedding
the spruce trees stood so contentedly on the sandy hill
and the pines so proudly on the steep precipice
and the junipers so happily on the sunny slope
and the little flowers all had white collars.
Then the forests dropped their seeds into human hearts,
the glittering lakes swam in human eyes
and the white butterflies fluttered ceaselessly by.

We Women

We women, we are so close to the brown earth.
We ask the cuckoo what he expects of the spring,
we throw our arms around the bare pine tree,
we search in the sunset for signs and counsel.
Once I loved a man, he believed in nothing . . .
He came one cold day with empty eyes,
he went one heavy day with forgetfulness on his brow.
If my child does not live, it is his . . .

Early Dawn

A few last stars glow exhaustedly.
I see them out of my window. The sky is pale,
one scarcely senses the day that is beginning in the distance.
There rests a silence spread out over the lake,
there lurks a whispering among the trees,
my old garden listens half-distraught
to the night's breathing that murmurs over the road.

Nordic Spring

All my castles of air have melted like snow,
all my dreams have run out like water,
of all that I loved I have only left
a blue sky and a few pale stars.
The wind moves softly among the trees.
The emptiness rests. The water is silent.
The old spruce tree stands awake and thinks
about the white cloud he kissed in a dream.

The Sorrowing Garden

Alas, that windows see
and walls remember,
that a garden can stand and sorrow
and a tree can turn round and ask:
Who has not come and what is not well,
why is the emptiness heavy and saying nothing?
The bitter carnations gather at the road,
there the spruce's darkness becomes unknowable.

Strange Sea

Strange fishes glide in the depths,
unfamiliar flowers glow on the shore;
I have seen red and yellow and all the other colours, –
but the gaudy gay sea is the most dangerous to look upon,
it makes one thirsty and wide-awake for waiting adventures:
what happened in the fairy-tale will happen also to me!

The Low Shore

The light birds high up in the air
do not fly for me,
but the heavy stones on the low shore
rest for me.
Long I lay at the feet of the dim hills
and listened to the wind's command
in the pine's strong branches.
Here I lie on my belly and look straight before me:
here all is strange and wakes no memories,
my thoughts were not born in this place;
here the air is raw and the stones slippery,
here all is dead and wakes no cheerfulness,
but for the broken flute the spring left on the shore.

The Song on the Rock

The sun went down over the foam of the sea and the shore
      slept
and up on the rocks someone stood and sang . . .
When the words fell into the water they were dead . . .
And the song disappeared behind the pines and the twilight
      took it with it.
When all was silent I thought only
that there lay heart's blood on the twilit cliff,
I sensed darkly that the song was
of something that never returns.

Evening

I do not want to hear the mournful tale
the forest tells.
There is still a whispering among the spruces,
there is still a sighing long in the leaves,
still long glide the shadows among the dim trunks.
Come out on the road. There no one will meet us.
The evening dreams pale red along silent ditches.
The road runs slowly and the road rises gently
and looks long round itself for the sun's gleam.

Foreign Lands

My soul loves foreign lands so much
as if it had no homeland.
In far-off lands stand the great stones
on which my thoughts rest.
It was a foreigner who wrote the strange words
on the hard board that is called my soul.
Days and nights I lie and think
about things that never happened:
my thirsty soul was once given a drink.

Do Not Let Your Pride Fall

Do not let your pride fall,
do not glide naked
into his arms tenderly,
rather go away in tears
the world has never seen
and never judged.
It would be easy and simple for the pure of heart
to follow happiness's tracks,
but our souls could only shiver.
For one who has seen the dirt in joy's brief spring
there remains nothing
but to freeze hotly to death.

Two Goddesses

When you saw the face of happiness you were disappointed:
that sleeping woman with loose features,
she was the most worshipped and the most often named,
the least known of all goddesses,
she who reigns over the becalmed seas,
the flowering gardens, the endless days of sunlight,
and you resolved never to serve her.

Nearer again with depth in her eyes again trod pain,
the never-invoked,
the best known and least understood of all goddesses,
she who reigns over the stormy seas and the sinking ships,
over the life prisoners,
and over the heavy curses that rest with the child in the
        mother's womb.

A Captured Bird

A bird sat captured in a golden cage
in a white castle by a deep blue sea.
Languishing roses promised pleasure and happiness.
And the bird sang of a little town high up in the mountains,
where the sun is king and silence queen
and where sparing little flowers in glowing colours
witness to life that defies and persists.

Farewell

Wilful and cold my heart has become
since I began to long for your caresses.
My sisters have not yet noticed
that I no longer look at them . . .
I will never speak to anyone any more . . .
I do not know how often
I kiss the little kitten that sleeps at my breast.
I should even like to be a little bored,
but my heart is happy and laughs at everything.

My sisters, I am doing what I never wanted to do,
my sisters, hold me back –
I do not want to go away from you.
When I close my eyes, he is standing before me,
I have many thoughts for him and none for all the others.
———————————————————————
My life has become as threatening as a stormy sky,
my life has become as false as mirroring water,
my life walks on a rope high up in the air:
I do not dare look at it.
All the desires I had yesterday
droop like the lowest leaves on the palm's stem,
all the prayers I said yesterday are superfluous and unanswered.
I have taken back all my words,
and all that I owned I have given away to the poor,
who wished me luck.

When I think properly
I have nothing left of myself but my black hair,
my two long tresses that glide like snakes.
My lips have become glowing coals,
I do not remember any more when they began to burn . . .
Terrible was the great fire that razed my girlhood to ashes.
O the inevitable must happen like a sword-cut –
I am going without farewell and unnoticed,
I am going utterly and will never return.

A Counsel

And the queen asked her secret counsellor:
Who is the wicked woman my husband loves?
– He loves all women who fire his blood. –
But which of these must I fight most?
– It is your own black temper you must fight most. –
But how shall I fight my own black temper?
– Let the messenger kiss you when the sun goes down. –

Sorrows

Sister fair, do not go up into the mountains: they deceived me,
they had nothing to give my longing.
As a keepsake I broke off a branch from the pine
that shadowed the road luxuriant as a plume,
and sought my way back to the sea in my old tracks.
The sea has broken thousands of toys and thrown them up on
        the sand –
in vain I seek an ornament to give my beauty brilliance.
Come, sit down with me, I shall tell you about my sorrows,
we shall talk with one another of secrets.
You will show me your beauty and your way of looking
and I shall offer you my silence and my custom of listening.

My Soul

My soul cannot tell stories and know any truth,
my soul can only weep and laugh and wring its hands;
my soul cannot reminisce and defend,
my soul cannot weigh over and confirm.
When I was a child I saw the sea: it was blue,
in my youth I met a flower: it was red,
now a foreigner sits by my side: he is without colour,
but I am not more fearful of him than the maiden was of the
        dragon.
When the knight came the maiden was red and white,
but I have dark rings under my eyes.

Love

My soul was a light blue dress of the sky's colour;
I left it on a rock beside the sea
and naked I came to you and resembled a woman.
And as a woman I sat at your table
and drank a bowl of wine and breathed in the scent of some
        roses.
You thought I was lovely and that I resembled someone you
        had seen in a dream,
I forgot everything, I forgot my childhood and my homeland,
I knew only that your caresses held me captive.
And smiling you took a mirror and bade me look at myself.
I saw that my shoulders were made of dust and fell apart,
I saw that my beauty was sick and had no will other than – to
        vanish.
O, hold me close in your arms so tightly that I need nothing.

The Mirroring Well

Destiny said: white you live or red you die!
But my heart resolved: red I live.
Now I live in the land where everything is yours,
death never enters this kingdom.
All day I sit resting my arm on the marble rim of the well,
when they ask me if happiness has been here
I shake my head and smile:
happiness is far away, where a young woman sits sewing a
      child's blanket,
happiness is far away, where a man builds himself a cabin in
      the forest.
Here red roses grow around bottomless wells,
here fine days mirror their smiling features
and great flowers lose their most beautiful petals . . .

The Song of the Three Graves

She sang in the dusk on the dew-wet courtyard:
Next summer three rose bushes grow above three graves.

In the first grave lies a man –
he sleeps heavily . . .

In the second lies a woman with sorrowful features –
she holds a rose in her hand.

The third grave is a spirit grave and is unblessed,
there every evening sits a dark angel singing: not to act is
      unforgivable.

The Foreign Tree

The foreign tree stands with gaudy fruits,
the foreign tree stands with purple catkins
on a sunny slope and whispers softly:
Come, come you golden daughter, you wanderer of autumn,
     you listener of the forest,
I shall tell you where happiness comes from and where
     happiness goes.
Lay your fingers on my bark and I shall
cover your limbs with autumn's glory.
Come, come you caresser, you faery one, you blessed, you
     red one,
I will show you the road that no one can find alone . . .
Come, come, you pale, you desirous of blood,
you shall go far away from here, to where no one knows you,
there you shall meet oriental eyes,
they ask never, they rest in melancholy . . .
You shall live far from your home and be happy.

Two Ways

You must give up your old way,
your way is dirty:
there men go with greedy glances
and the word "happiness" you hear from every lip
and further along the way lies the body of a woman
and the vultures are tearing it to pieces.

You have found your new way,
your way is pure:
there motherless children go playing with poppies,
there women in black go talking of sorrow
and further along the way stands a pale saint
with his foot on a dead dragon's neck.

Three Sisters

The first sister loved sweet strawberries,
the second sister loved red roses,
the third sister loved the wreaths of the dead.

The first sister got married:
they say that she is happy.

The second sister loved with all her soul,
they say that she was unhappy.

The third sister became a saint,
they say that she will win the crown of eternal life.

Christian Confession

Happiness is not what we dream of,
happiness is not the night we remember,
happiness is not in our yearning's song.

Happiness is something we never wanted,
happiness is something we find it hard to understand,
happiness is the cross that was raised for everyone.

Beauty

What is beauty? Ask every soul –
beauty is every overflow, every glow, every overfilling and
      every great poverty;
beauty is to be faithful to the summer and to go naked until
      the autumn;
beauty is the plumage of the parrot or the sunset that bodes
      storms;
beauty is a sharp feature and an accent of one's own: it is I,
beauty is a great loss and a silent funeral procession,

beauty is the fan's light beat that wakes the breeze of
        destiny:
beauty is to be as voluptuous as the rose
or to forgive everything because the sun is shining;
beauty is the cross the monk chose or the necklace the lady
        has from her lover,
beauty is not the thin sauce in which poets serve themselves,
beauty is to wage war and seek happiness,
beauty is to serve higher powers.

The King's Sorrow

The king had the word "sorrow" forbidden at court,
"ill-luck", "love" and "luck" that all hurt,
but "she" and "hers" still remained.
His queen caressed him like a child,
in the twilight hours he lay at her breast
his eyes wide with pain.
He listened in fear to every footstep that approached the
        door,
and reluctance spread over his face.
If maidens laughed in the courtyard like silver springs,
the king grew pale and changed the subject.
No young woman with blond locks
dared show herself any longer with uncovered head,
and the little dancing-girls in short skirts
were all banned from the court.
When the spring came the king did not go out in the garden,
he lay on his bed facing north . . .
The spring looked pale blue in through the window panes.

Life's Sister

Life looks most like death, her sister.
Death is not different,
you can caress her and hold her hand and smooth her hair,
she will hand you a flower and smile.

78

You can bore your face into her breast
and hear her say: it is time to go.
She will tell you that she is another.
Death does not lie green-white with her face to the ground
or on her back on a white bier:
death walks about with pink cheeks and talks to everyone.
Death has weak features and saintly cheeks,
upon your heart she lays her soft hand.
Whoever feels that soft hand on his heart,
the sun does not warm him,
he is as cold as ice and loves no one.

From 'Tales of Lilliput'

At last the lazybones got up –
he sank his hand into the chalice of every flower,
he felt under every leaf,
he sought the black worm to kill him.
But when he was asleep in the shadow of a stem of grass
the black worm ate up his head.
Three women were present at his burial:
his sister wept; with her was a dancing-girl in heliotrope veils,
she had come in order to be seen.
Alone walked a woman he had never loved.

On the Shore

When it rains and the sea is grey I grow sick . . .
I laugh with the sun, I drive with the wind, I chaff with the sea:
high seas are the only thing I love.
I live in a cave with many bats,
but I am fine and white with deceitful eyes.

My feet are the loveliest I have seen,
I wash them perpetually in water and foam.
My hands are beautiful and dazzling,
I shine like the whole cheerful and smiling coastline.
Wanderers that go past I look in the eye
so that they grow forlorn and restless for the rest of their lives.
Alas, but when I prop my head up in my hands
what is it that always hurts so much?
I knocked myself so hard against a rock that time I nearly died,
because I stretched out my arm in vain
towards a foreigner I saw once . . .

Life

I, my own prisoner, say so:
life is not the springtime clad in light green velvet,
or a caress that one seldom receives,
life is not a resolve to go
or two white arms that hold one back.
Life is the narrow ring that holds us captive,
the invisible circle we never cross,
life is nearby happiness that passes us by,
and the thousand steps we cannot bring ourselves to take.
Life is to despise oneself
and to lie motionless on the bottom of a well
and to know that the sun is shining up there
and golden birds are flying through the air
and the days swift as arrows are shooting by.
Life is to wave a short farewell and go home and sleep . . .
Life is to be a foreigner to oneself
and a new mask for every other person who comes.
Life is to be careless with one's own happiness
and to push away the unique moment,
life is to think oneself weak and not to dare.

Hell

O how wonderful is hell!
In hell no one speaks of death.
Hell is built in the bowels of the earth
and adorned with glowing flowers . . .
In hell no one speaks an empty word . . .
In hell no one has drunk and no one has slept
and no one rests and no one sits still.
In hell no one speaks, but everyone screams,
there tears are not tears and all sorrows are without strength.
In hell no one is ill and no one is tired.
Hell is immutable and eternal.

The Waiting Soul

I am alone amidst the trees at the lake's edge,
I live in friendship with the shore's old firs
and in secret understanding with all the young rowans.
Alone I lie and wait,
I have seen no one walk by.
Great flowers look down on me from tall stems,
bitter creepers climb in my embrace,
I have a single name for everything, and that is love.

Pain

Happiness has no songs, happiness has no thoughts, happinesss
        has nothing.
Smash your happiness in pieces, for happiness is evil.
Happiness comes softly with the mornings murmuring in
        sleeping thickets,
happiness glides away in light cloud-pictures over deep-blue
        deeps,
happiness is the field asleep in the glow of midday
or the sea's infinite expanse in the bask of vertical rays,

happiness is powerless, she sleeps and breathes and knows of
        nothing . . .
Do you know pain? She is strong and great with secretly
        clenched fists.
Do you know pain? She smiles hopefully with eyes swollen
        from weeping.
Pain gives us all that we need –
she gives us the keys to the kingdom of death,
she pushes us in through the gate while we still hesitate.
Pain baptises the child and awakes with the mother
and forges all the golden wedding rings.
Pain rules over all, she smooths the thinker's brow,
she fastens the necklace around the neck of the desired woman,
she stands in the doorway when the man leaves his true love . . .
What more does pain give her darlings?
I know no more.
She gives pearls and flowers, she gives songs and dreams,
she gives us a thousand kisses that are all empty,
she gives us the only kiss that is real.
She gives us our strange souls and curious likings,
she gives us all life's highest gains:
love, solitude, and the face of death.

EARLY POEMS FROM
The Land That Is Not

Summer in the Mountains

The mountains' summer is simple:
the meadow flowers,
the old courtyard smiles
and the beck's dark murmur speaks of happiness found.

The Rose

I am beautiful, for I have grown in my beloved's garden.
I stood in spring rain and got yearning to drink,
I stood in the sun and got heat to drink –
now I stand open and wait.

A Sick Visit

I bring you a single blossom-laden branch
out of the spring's great forest.
You are silent and you look down
with your sick deep eyes
at the light's reflection in the crystal vases.
You are silent and you smile,
for this spring will pass your heart by.
We have nothing any more to say.

The Portrait

For my little songs,
the amusingly complaining, the evening red,
the spring gave me the egg of a waterfowl.

I asked my beloved to paint my portrait on the thick shell.
He painted a young bulb in brown soil –
and on the other side a round soft mound of sand.

A Meeting

Three maidens walked hand in hand across an open plain.
They were met by a horseman in the dense mist.
The first maiden stretched out her arms: love has come!
The second maiden fell to her knees: death spare me!
The third maiden turned around:
the road to the city branches off to the right.

Night Madonna

When the black clouds marched across the sky
a mother sat awake and a child slept.
And an angel's voice sang in the night's silence
the praise of all the worlds.

And the young mother heard like an echo
most deeply within her the night's silent praise:
O how the world grew out to every latitude
while the little one slept!

In Autumn

Now it is autumn and the golden birds
are all flying homewards across deep blue waters;
I sit on the shore and stare at the gaudy glitter
and the farewell soughs in the branches.
The farewell is great, the parting is near,
but the return meeting is certain.
Therefore my sleep grows light when I sleep with my arm
        under my head.
I feel a mother's breathing on my eyes
and a mother's mouth against my heart:
sleep and slumber, my child, for the sun has gone. –

Dangerous Dreams

Do not go too near your dreams:
they are a smoke and they could blow away –
they are dangerous and could endure.

Have you looked your dreams in the eye?
They are sick and understand nothing –
they have only their own thoughts.

Do not go too near your dreams:
they are an untruth, they ought to go –
they are a madness, they want to stay.

.

The Bride

My circle is narrow and the ring of my thoughts
fits round my finger.
There lies something warm at the ground of all the foreignness
        around me,
like the weak scent in the chalice of the water-lily.
A thousand apples hang in my father's garden,
round and complete in themselves –
so my undetermined life has been
formed, rounded, swelling and smooth and – simple.
Narrow is my circle and the ring of my thoughts
fits round my finger.

To Eros

Eros, you cruellest of all gods,
why have you led me into the dark land?
When girl children grow up
they are shut out from the light
and flung into a dark room.
Did my soul not float like a lucky star
before it was drawn into your red orbit?

See, I am bound hand and foot,
feel, I am forced to all my thoughts.
Eros, you cruellest of all gods:
I do not flee, I do not wait,
I only suffer like a beast.

The Princess

Every evening the princess let herself be caressed.
But the one who caresses merely stills his own hunger
and her yearning was a shy mimosa, a wide-eyed fairy-tale in
        the presence of reality.
New caresses filled her heart with bitter sweetness
and her body with ice, but her heart wanted even more.
The princess knew bodies, but she sought hearts;
she had never seen another heart besides her own.

The princess was the poorest in the whole kingdom:
she had lived too long on illusions.
She knew that her heart must die and be utterly destroyed,
for truth corrodes.
The princess did not love the red mouths, they were foreign.
The princess did not notice the drunken eyes with ice at the
        bottom.
They were all children of winter, but the princess was from
        the far south and without fickleness,
without hardness, without veils and without cunning.

My Future

A fickle moment
stole my future from me,
future haphazardly put together.
I shall build it up much better
just as I imagined it to start with.
I shall build it up on the firm field
that is called my will.

I shall raise it up on the tall pillars
that are called my ideals.
I shall build it with a mysterious secret passage
that is called my soul.
I shall build it with a high tower
that is called aloneness.

Sick Days

My heart is kept wedged in a narrow cleft,
far away my heart is placed
on a distant island.
White birds fly to and fro
bringing the news that my heart is alive.
I know how it lives –
on coal and sand
upon sharp stones.

I lie all day on my back and wait for the night,
I lie all night and wait for the day,
I lie sick in the garden of paradise.
I know that I will not get better,
longing and pining do not get better.
I have fever like a marsh plant,
I sweat sweetness like a sticky leaf.

At the bottom of my garden lies a sleepy lake.
I who love the earth
know nothing better than water.
Into the water fall all my thoughts
that no one has seen,
my thoughts that I do not dare to show to anyone.
The water is full of secrets!

Nothing

Be still, my child, nothing is there,
and all is as you see: forest, smoke, and the flight of the
      railway tracks.

Somewhere far away in a distant land
there is a bluer sky and a wall with roses
or a palm tree and a warmer wind –
and that is all.
There is nothing more than the snow on the spruce-fir's bough.
There is nothing to kiss with warm lips,
and all lips cool with time.
But you say, my child, that your heart is powerful,
and that living in vain is inferior to dying.
What did you want of death? Do you know the disgust his
          clothes spread?
And nothing is more revolting than death by one's own hand.
We ought to love life's long hours of sickness
and narrow years of longing
like the brief moments when the desert flowers.

A Life

The stars are relentless –
we all know that –
but I will seek happiness on all blue waves
and under all grey stones.
If happiness never comes? What is a life?
A little water-lily withers away in the sand.
And if its instinct fails it? A tide dies on the shore
when the sun goes down.
What had the fly to seek in the spider's web,
and what has the mayfly done with its single day?
There is no answer save two lifeless wings
over a sunken breast.
Black never becomes white –
yet the struggle's sweetness remains for all
and on all days fresh flowers come from hell.
But there comes a day when hell is empty and heaven is locked
and all stands still –
then nothing remains but a mayfly's body in the fold of a leaf.
But no one knows it any more.

The Miracle

THE GIRL:
I was so happy when I saw you, O sister,
I was so happy that there was someone in the forest
besides mocking echoes and lurking trolls.
You walked so slowly, I hurried after you
to catch you up, as though I had something to tell you.
Lustreless and severe is the black nun's dress,
gravity peers out of the dark folds,
but it is dear and intimate and marvellously consoling
to hearts that carry secret sorrows.

———————————————————————————

Alas sister, sister, the velvet green forest is glorious,
but this spring is no spring for me.
For the one I loved has done me wrong.
He took my love with cunning like a betrayer
for the sake of his base and ignoble vanity,
and left me alone in sorrow and shame in cold contempt.
Heavy my heart has been all the time that the sun has not
          warmed me.

Now I have dreamt two nights in a row
that I was happy and carried a knife in my hand,
a bloody knife, and my heart was as light as a bird.
Dreams mean nothing, but I wonder
if I shall see the same dream one more time.

THE NUN:
You must not dream so, my child,
you must not dream so one more time.
Now is the holy season of leaf-burst
when the earth is full of angels,
and whoever listens will hear the constant beat of wings in the air.
Now is the holy season of leaf-burst,
when angels light the candles in the church
and fill the bowls with holy baptismal water,
and above the altar stands the Mother of God
with an imperceptible smile on her lips.
Go thither, fall down upon your knees . . . and wait.
Alas, when the Mother of God looks down at you
you will feel it at once.

90

I know it well. How the pain gently subsides –
within an hour you will have forgotten your sorrows
and your thoughts will become light and bright and still
like angels' footsteps over the floor of stone,
and you will arise and hurry involuntarily towards the exit,
tears will flood over your face
and you will be blissful and slightly sunken about your lips,
and at night you will dream blissfully and piously
as children dream on Christmas Eve.
Go into the church, my child, I shall wait out here in quiet prayer.

THE GIRL *(returning)*:
How...heavy...is my mind.
Weak are your prayers, O sister,
the holy baptismal water did not work.
I kneeled before the altar,
long I kept my eyes closed and thought nothing
expecting the miracle.
Would that I had never opened my eyes!
I saw it again . . . what I saw in my dream . . .
yet it was a thousand times more ominous to see it
here on the holy altar.
On the floor I saw some drops of blood,
a stripe of clotted blood on the altar cloth,
but up on the altar lay – the knife.
I wanted to grasp it and kiss it –
what is there in the world I love like this blood?
The floor swayed strangely beneath my knees,
a terror took me – I remembered the Mother of God
and I looked up to her with a prayer for forgiveness
and sought her protection.
But she did not see me, she looked out into the distance
terrible and aloof.

———————————————————————

In vain are all prayers for me.

THE NUN:
Yet I shall pray for you,
now I will never cease to pray for you.
The Mother of God does not see you, she is silent . . .
She wants a sacrifice compared with which all sacrifices are petty.
She, the holy and pure, against whom all evil is powerless

91

takes as a sacrifice out of your hands
the heavy knife with the evil blood.
Great is her mercy,
deep is her pity,
her thoughts are higher than men's laws.
She does not kill the evil thoughts when they are brought to
      birth,
she does not stem the evil words that stream over lips,
she does not check the uplifted arm when the blow falls.
But for the crushed souls, over which misfortune has passed,
she has a mercy without bounds and a love without distinction.
She gives us tears that melt our hearts
and make them soft as wax.
Thus is the Mother of God
and little do we know her.
She sees all that come here,
and various is her mercy towards all.
But only the heaviest hearts
weigh anything in her hand.
Great will be the sweetness of your remorse, my child,
when the evil thing has happened.
Always I have lived far from evil,
my soul has been bright as the white lily
the tall angel holds in his hand.
Yet I have taught myself that there is nothing good
far from sin.
What is the necessity of our prayers?
The strength of despair that overpowers our saints?
Do we need the Mother of God? Could we not live without her?
We are not ready for paradise:
the pure souls should be thrown into the fire and ought to burn.
Stunted are all hearts that do not flower freely.
Cautious are our souls in their white attire.
There are too many in the world
who merit being called cowardly.
But blessed are those souls
in which evil has lost its greatest investment:
Go my child, I shall pray for you.
I can do no other.

[1915]

The September Lyre (1918)

Introductory Note

That my writing is poetry no one can deny, that is is verse I will not insist. I have attempted to bring certain refractory poems under one rhythm and have thereby discovered that I possess the power of the word and the image only under conditions of complete freedom, i.e. at the expense of the rhythm. My poems are to be taken as careless pencil sketches. As regards the content, I let my instinct build up what my intellect sees in expectation. My self-confidence depends on the fact that I have discovered my dimensions. It does not become me to make myself less than I am.

Author.

Triumph of being . . .

What have I to fear? I am a part of infinity.
I am a part of the all's great power,
a lonely world inside millions of worlds,
like a star of the first degree that fades last.
Triumph of living, triumph of breathing, triumph of being!
Triumph of feeling time run ice-cold through one's veins
and of hearing the silent river of the night
and of standing on the mountain under the sun.
I walk on sun, I stand on sun,
I know of nothing else than sun.

Time—convertress, time—destructress, time—enchantress,
do you come with new schemes, a thousand tricks to offer
        me existence
as a little seed, as a coiled snake, as a rock amidst the sea?
Time – you murderess – leave me!
The sun fills my breast with sweet honey up to the brim
and she says: all stars fade at last, but they always shine
        without fear.

[1916]

To a Young Woman

A fiery glance has never yet betrayed.
Hold the man's heart in your unversed child's fingers,
draw the man's streaming fire into the icy staterooms of
        your eyes!
You are as certain of love as you are of the kingdom of heaven.
He will give you his heart, a kingdom and all the flowers of spring,
and you will give him the light veil of your longing that makes
        the distance blue.
Still your breath has not touched the fluttering light of his bliss.
Still your eye has not measured the extent of his faith.
Still your feet have not crossed into the closed circle of his
        destiny;
it is still the same to you whether it is red or blue.

95

But there will come a day when you hang close
to him like a flower to its stem,
when his dusk is your light and his drought is your spring,
when you wander around the passages of a wide-flung castle
        and know that you love
and that he only lives on the white bread of your purity
and that his blood only streams in the basin of your motherly
        tenderness.
All will be heavy and miraculous and hard and indivisible.

[1916]

Dusk

Night is coming tall in his fleecy beard,
smiling a whole smile to the half-veiled world.
Formless, gigantic, out of the dumb lilacs
grow the contours of the park in the dusk.
The pretty lilacs have sleepy ears,
they are dreaming that the sun is coming down to earth . . .
What can a dreamlike dusk do against all the waking thoughts
that steal by unseen . . .

[1916]

Revelation

Your love is darkening my star –
the moon is rising in my life.
My hand is not at home in yours.
Your hand is lust –
my hand is longing.

[1916]

96

Strong Hyacinths

You will not get me to believe in disgusting flies
– revenge and petty lusts.
I believe in strong hyacinths that drip the scent of ages.
Lilies are healing and pure as my own sharpness.
You will not get me to believe in disgusting flies
that gather stink and plague.
I believe that great stars are making way for my desire –
somewhere between sun and south, between north and night.

[1916]

What Is Tomorrow?

What is tomorrow? Perhaps not you.
Perhaps another's arms and a new contact and a similar pain...
I shall leave you with a certainty like no other:
I shall come back as a fragment of your own pain.
I shall come to you from another sky with a new resolve.
I shall come to you from another star with the same look.
I shall come to you with my old longing in new features.
I shall come to you strange, angry and faithful
with the footfalls of a wild beast out of your heart's far desert
        homeland.
You will fight against me hard and powerlessly
as one only fights against one's destiny, against one's luck,
        against one's star.
I shall smile and bind silken threads around my finger
and I shall hide the little spool of your destiny in the folds of
        my clothes.

The Death of the Maiden

The soul of the pure maiden was never mistaken,
she knew everything about herself,
she knew even more: about others and about the sea.
Her eyes were bilberries, her lips cranberries, her hands wax.
she crouched and whirled and fell – and faded away.
When she was gone no one knew that her body still lay in the
        forest . . .
They sought her long among the maidens on the seashore,
that sang of little mussels in red shells.
They sought her long among drunken men,
who quarrelled about shiny knives in the duke's kitchen.
They sought her long in the field of lilies-of-the-valley,
her shoe had remained there since the previous night.

[Christmas Eve 1916]

The Little Old Man

The little old man sits counting eggs.
Each time he counts there is one egg less.
Do not show him your gold my friends.

The Tree in the Forest

There once grew a tree in the forest –
so beautiful and strong –
I had seen it . . .
It rose over the mists of the deep to the summits of the earth in
        solitary radiance.
———————————————————————————
Now I am told that lightning has struck it . . .
What can one do
about thunder's destruction and lightning's bolts?
I have indeed seen this tree in the forest
and shall remember it
as long as songs keep their roots.

Grimace d'Artiste

I have nothing other than my glowing cape,
my red lack of fear.
My red lack of fear goes out adventuring
in petty lands.

I have nothing other than my lyre under my arm,
my hard harp-playing;   .
my hard lyre sounds for man and beast
on open roads.

I have nothing other than my high borne crown,
my rising pride.
My rising pride takes the lyre under its arm
and bows farewell.

The Bull

Where is the bull?
My character is a red rag.
I see no blood-exploded eyes,
I hear no short, fiery breathing,
is the ring not quaking under furious hooves?
No.
The bull has no horns;
he stands at the manger
and stubbornly chews his tough hay.
Unpunished the reddest rag flutters in the wind.

Prayer

God, thou all-powerful, take pity on us!
Look into our worship's well – it wants to grow deeper.
Seven days and seven nights
we fetch up water
from our well for thee.

99

Seven months and three years
in the same place
we beg for thy mercy:
give us entry to the silent chamber where thou thinkest about
    things.

[1918]

O my sunflame-coloured peaks . . .

O my sunflame-coloured peaks,
will you take me back?
Eternally I want to live in your lonely pleasure garden.
There alone is my home,
there fire-eyed angels
falling to their knees
kiss away all longing's dew from earth.

O my undarkened peaks!
Not a day do I live far from you,
unblessed I should perish.
The earth die for me on the third day,
its forests murmur out of a dream for me.
What are bridges, fields and towns to me?
Stains on your clean blue sky,
shadow in your bright eye, day,
howl of wolves from an abyss.

O my sunflame-coloured peaks –
– could I exchange a world against my strength?
If I heal myself
this drop is enough for all that breathes.
Therefore, longing, brace thyself!
Will, grow high up into the clouds!
Arise ye, bold warriors,
aerial and merry as armed devils!
— — — — — — — — — — — — — — — — — — —
White earth and high heaven
we lay at your feet, sunflame-coloured peaks.

[1918]

The World Is Bathing in Blood

The world is bathing in blood because God had to live.
In order that his glory may persist, all other must perish.
What do we human beings know of how the eternal one
      languishes
and what the gods drink to feed their strength?
God wants to create anew. He wants to reform the world to
      a clearer sign.
Therefore he girds himself with a belt of lightnings,
therefore he bears a crown of blazing thorns,
therefore he shrouds the earth in blindness and night.
Therefore his gaze is cruel. His creator's hands squeeze the
      earth mightily.
What it is he creates no one knows. But it moves like a dread
over half-awake senses. It is like a vertigo at the sight of abysses.
Before joyous choirs burst out into a song of praise
it is silent as in the forest before the sun rises.

The Storm

People,
is not a storm raging across the sky
raised up by your longing
borne by eagles
to incorruptible heights?
Whom will the storm force to his knees?
Where does he strike down,
he that is come from the heights, free, with the wings of
      far-distant times?
Do you hear
voices in the storm?
Helmets of Mars in the mist . . .
Guests sit down again at upturned tables.
Strangers rule the world . . .
Higher, more beautiful, godlike.

[1918]

Evening Walk

All the age's golden stars on my dark velvet dress.
I have triumphed . . . this evening . . . I shiver.
Destiny's iron bars hammer out of my breast.
Is the wind whirling sand from the pavement?
— —
Is there for me a death, annihilation? – no.
Death is in Helsinki –
he catches the sparks on the roofs.
I cross the square with my future in my breast.

The Moon's Secret

The moon knows . . . that blood will be shed here tonight.
On tracks of copper over the lake a certainty goes forth:
corpses shall lie amidst the alders on a wonderfully beautiful
        shore.
The moon shall cast its most beautiful light on the strange
        shore.
The wind shall pass like a wakening bugle call between the pines:
How beautiful is the earth in this lonely hour.

The Song from off the Cloud

Up on the clouds lives all that I need:
my daylight-proof hunches, my flashbulb certainties,
and on the clouds I live myself
– white, in sun that blinds,
inaccessibly happy, waving farewell.
Fare ye well, my youth's green forests.
Monsters run amok there –
I shall never set foot on earth again.
An eagle took me up on his wings –
far from the world
I have peace.
Up on the clouds I sit and sing –

102

down on the earth drips quicksilver mocking laughter –
out of it grow tickle-grass and fly-in-the-air flowers.

[1918]

The Whirlpool of Madness

Guard your boat from superhuman currents,
from the whirlpool abyss of madness –
guard your boat from ruin's exultant waves,
they break apart.
Guard yourself – here you no longer matter –
life and death are one before the frenetic joy of power,
here there is no "slow", "careful", "try".
Stronger hands than yours grasp your oar in flight.
There you yourself stand, a heroine with reborn blood.
Ravished in calm, a bonfire of joy on mirroring ice,
as if death's message were not written for you:
blessed waves lead your keel onwards.

[1918]

Sunset Landscape

See in the sunset
floating islands of fire parading
imperially over cream-green seas.
Islands aflame! Islands like torches!
Islands in victory parade!
Up out of the deep a forest lightens blackly
slyly, enviously – ravished, displaying itself, triumph to triumph...
Poor streaks of forest in pale mists
are seized, lifted up – unite themselves to majesty.

Glory! Victory!
Fall down on bended knees, leonine monsters,
in dim corners of the world.

103

The day goes enthroned to its end . . .
Light's threads are cut off by invisible hands.

[1918]

Revanche

If I do not succeed in toppling
this tower in reality's citadel,
I will sing down the stars from heaven
as no one else has ever done.
I will sing so that my longing ceases,
longing that never has known rest,
that it may push the lyre aside
as if the song's task were at an end.

[1918]

The Fairy's Castle

Behind the sea begin the mountains,
behind the mountains lies the fairy's castle in the clouds.
The fairy is never more than fifteen years old. –
Her dress of sunshine is more costly than the earth.
The fairy wills that all shall be as blissful as herself . . .
she wants to give away her light heart to those who meet her.
Be transformed,
the fairy has touched you with her wand.

[1918]

The Footsteps of the Gods

The gods go through life with their hearts high above pain . . .
The gods bear life lightly as pillars bear radiant vaults.
The gods go through life alone, unrecognized they stand and
    look out of eternal eyes at our dim earth.

104

And where they have gazed out across forest and lake
there are trees and water holy.
Where they have wandered it is a balm for those to walk
who struggle with pain-heavy breast.
Where they have wandered it is a joy for those to walk
who stride their victor's paths.
The footsteps of the gods do not vanish from the world;
that they walk over it makes the earth high
and makes everything pardonable to human beings.

[1918]

The Lyre of the Gods

Where is the lyre
of silver and ivory
that gods have lent
the race of mortals?
It has not been lost,
for eternal gifts
are not worn out by time,
do not perish in fire.

But if a singer approaches
marked out by destiny,
he grasps it anew
from forgotten vaults.
And when he tunes it
the whole world knows
that the gods are alive
on unsuspected heights.

The Mother of God's Rose

There lies a rose in the arms of the Mother of God.
A petal thereof
heals sick hearts.

There lies a rose in the arms of the Mother of God.
Radiant-eyed, she smiles –
who wants to heal his own venomous heart?

The Condition

Without action
I cannot live,
chained to the lyre I should die.
The lyre is the highest thing I know upon earth
and I would remain faithful to it
were I not a blazing soul.
Whoever does not make his breach
with bloody nails in the wall of everyday
– may perish outside it –
he is not fit to see the sun.

[September 1918]

The Spirit of the Apocalypse
(*Fragment*)

People, there is a heaving in my breast.
Fire, smoke, the stench of burnt flesh:
it is the war.

— — — — — — — — — — — — — — — — — — — —

Out of the war have I come – risen out of chaos –
I am the elements – biblically riding – the apocalypse.
I look around across life – it is godlike.
The war is mine – your silent master's armed millions
who needed you? The deeps gape.
Unsayable things are happening behind the veils of destiny.

Doubters, mockers,
do not lay a finger on life's mystery.
Life is godlike and for children.

— — — — — — — — — — — — — — — — — —

The singers were no harpists,
no – disguised gods – spies of God.
Singers of bygone times – be consoled,
good blood has flowed in your veins –
most abundant red blood of warriors.
The spirit of the song is the war.

[September 1918]

The Armoured Train

Fifty waggons full of hopes I had loaded to your America.
They came back empty . . .
Freight of deception . . .
Now I send armoured trains with stone-hard masks in
        menacing embrasures:
they come home with thousandfold waggons of fulfilment.

[September 1918]

The Trains of the Future

Tear down all the triumphal arches –
the triumphal arches are too low.
Make room for our fantastic trains!
Heavy is the future – build the bridges
to the limitless.
Giants, bring stones from the ends of the world!
Demons, pour oil under the boilers!
Monster, do the measurements with your tail!
Arise into the heavens, heroic forms,
hands swollen with destiny – begin your work.
Break off a piece of heaven. Red hot.
We must scratch and fight.
We must struggle for the manna of the future.
Arise, heralds,
who are already strangely visible from afar,
the day needs a cock-crow.

Freedom from Sorrow

I do not believe in human beings.
I would have smashed my lyre in pieces
if I had not believed in God.
God shows me the way
out of the mist towards the sun's radiant disc.
He loves the light-footed wanderers.
Therefore he gave me all this freedom from sorrow.
I trust in him as in a rock.
If I am his true child – then nothing can befall me.

[September 1918]

The Fields of Light

I have powers. I fear nothing.
The sky is light for me.
If the world ends –
I will not end.
My light horizons stand
above the earth's storming night.
Come forth out of the enigmatic, fields of light!
Inflexible waits my power.

[September 1918]

Foam

Life's champagne
bubbling we drink
light as foam
champagne-hearts . . .

Champagne-eyes –
the sky winks promises to you

108

Champagne-feet –
follow the stars

Champagne-spirits
the glass is ecstatic in your hands!

[September 1918]

At Nietzsche's Grave

The great hunter is dead . . .
I drape his grave with warm curtains of flowers . . .
Kissing the cold stone, I say:
your first child is here in tears of joy.
Mockingly I sit on your grave
like a slap in the face – more beautiful than in your dreams.
Strange father!
Your children will not let you down,
they are coming across the earth with the footsteps of gods,
rubbing their eyes: where am I?
No, really . . . here is my place,
here is the run-down grave of my father . . .
Gods – keep eternal watch over this spot.

[September 1918]

The Most Beautiful God

My heart is the most beautiful thing in the world.
It is holy.
Whoever sees it
must reflect its brilliance.
My heart is light as a bird,
a more fragilely formed thing has never been found on earth.
I offer it in sacrifice
to an unknown god.
The god highest up in the clouds –

my wings will carry me there –
the most beautiful god
before whom everything is dust.
I shall return
with a shimmer around my forehead –
no one shall see anything else
than night and god.

[September 1918]

The Dawn

I light my light over all the Atlantic . . .
Unknown worlds, nocturnal lands
awake unto me!
I am the cold dawn,
I am the pitiless goddess of the day
in mist-grey veils
with a slight flashing of morning's helmet.
Light, light course my winds over the seas.
My powerful horn hangs at my side, I do not sound the
    departure . . .
Shall I wait even longer? Has a god fallen dreaming?
The morning rises red out of the ocean.

[September 1918]

Do Not Gather Gold and Precious Stones

People,
do not gather gold and precious stones:
fill your hearts with longing,
that burns like glowing coals.
Steal the rubies from the angels' eyes,
drink cold water from the devil's pool.

110

People, do not gather treasures
which make you into beggars;
gather riches
which give you the power of kings.
Give your children a beauty
which human eyes have never seen,
give your children the strength
to force the gates of heaven.

[September 1918]

If I Am a Liar

If I am a criminal, my sin cannot be measured . . .
If I am a jester, I jest with holy things . . .
If I am a liar, may I plunge down from heaven
crushed on your market-square.

If I am a liar –
may damned souls bury my lyre
in stagnant mires of sulphur,
may it stretch out beseeching arms on moonlit nights
in a place where no living thing passes.

If I am a liar –
may my wonderful name be erased from the wall of heaven,
may the letters of pearl be smashed on the rocks of the sea,
may the waters be silent about where I have come from,
may the world never hear my tale.

If I am a liar –
the beautiful angels will love me all the same
as a beautiful and unfortunate brother:
she told stories to the moon and the firmament,
without them they could not endure,
their fragile beauty fall to pieces.

[September 1918]

The Sign

Is god a villain?
Has he driven out his boldest angel from heaven?
No – I say:
He gave me honey and wormwood.
I threw the foaming mixture out over the earth.
        The cake-mould held.
He gave me a black-red rose –
the smallest in the world.
It marks me out from other human beings,
it can be seen from far off on my white dress.

[September 1918]

The Song of the Troubadour

Strange moon!
Within an hour it has risen –
gilding everything
with African reveries.
I stand with my lute
in the darkness of the courtyard.
The king's daughter in the tower
throws stars over me.
Then the forest lake smiles too –
O pearls, gold and silver! –
the sharp points cut in
like eternal memories.
I measure the bricks with my hand,
laughing with scorn:
Day, what more have you to bring
after night's song?

[September 1918]

My Lyre

I hate the thought . . .
Where is my beloved giant lyre?
Strung with sunshine, fairy-like, suspended from the clouds.
O my giant lyre,
you hang over the world like a question-mark.
————————————————————————————

When I die
I will throw myself carelessly onto your strings;
then two spirits will arise out of the unknown,
sleeping they will carry us above the seas,
they will stop in mid-Atlantic. –
————————————————————————————

And we will both have disappeared from the world,
my beloved lyre!

[September 1918]

Why Was Life Given Me?

Why was life given me,
to lighten past everyone in a triumphal chariot
as impossible to catch up with as destiny
willy-nilly,
longing for more?

Why was life given me,
to take the shimmering bowl,
conjured up,
with ring-bedecked hands,
thirsting for more?

Why was life given me,
to pass like a magic book from hand to hand
burning through every soul,
driving like a fire over ashes,
thirsting for more?

Fragment

— —
— —
— — — — life's bacteria thrive on your mucous membrane.
City, you wisely arched one, you have not broken my heart:
all your people come from the steppes,
even the greyest, most silent, saddest steppes
are open to the wind.
City, you suffering one, you are as gentle as a saint,
city, you suffocating, agonizing one, you have deeps   .
where we deep-sea fish can breathe.
Petersburg, Petersburg,
from your pinnacles flutters the magic flag of my childhood.

That was the time before the deep sores, before the terrible scars,
before rejuvenation's bath of oblivion.
Petersburg, Petersburg,
on your pinnacles the glow of my girlhood lies
like a pink drapery, like a light overture,
like the gauze of dreams over the sleep of giants.
Petersburg, Petersburg,
rise up out of golden visions!
What I love I will gather together in words torn loose.
I scatter the violets of memory on the golden pavements of
        dreams.
— —
What is happening to me as I speak?
Do I sense rightly the approach of immeasurable tragedies?
Do my fairy-tale viaducts never rise above your roofs,
do the trains not flash by with ecstatic pennants
to Berlin – Paris – London?
Will all that I see become a measureless ash-heap?
Or are these only clouds of tiredness passing?
Is our miraculous citadel not rising up out of the sea in Helsinki?
Are not watchmen standing there with blue and red flags the
        world has never seen?
Are they not standing, leaning on their spears, spying out the sea
with the granite of destiny in their petrified features?

114

Or is everything merely a mirror-reflection in sleepwalker's eyes,
do I live in a dream on another planet?

— — — — — — — — — — — — — — — — — — — —

Heaven itself wants to come down to earth.
Love nothing but infinity! is its first commandment.
Dream of nothing less than of kissing God's little finger.

— — — — — — — — — — — — — — — — — — — —

Children down there, loading dung onto the carts of the rabble,
on your knees! Do penance! Do not approach the holy
       thresholds yet –

Zarathustra is waiting in there for chosen guests.

Friends, we are as low as worms in the dust.
Not one row of us will stand before the gaze of the future.
With all the past we shall plunge into Lethe.
The future is rich, what have we to give from our beggars'
       rubbish?
The future walks over us with his victor's heels.
We are not worthy that the crosses should remain on our graves.

— — — — — — — — — — — — — — — — — — — —

Friends, I prophesy a feast in beauty's sign . . .
Where can it be if not in Engadin?
The old farms stand and look:
'From where has this beauty come to us?
From where a foreign, terrible, destroying spirit with
       boundless wings,
bringing sorrow and melancholy, farewell and death,
Beauty's restless, greedy, demanding spirit . . .
Destroying our gaudy flowers. Smashing the window in which
       the geraniums stand.
No idyllic paths lead any more to hundred-year homes,
the road of the demons is another, the march of the demons
is the heartless flight of the suns through space.
Eternal Fohn wind leaves not a stone intact on our roofs,
the storm will not cease upon earth . . .
Childbed and graves, shooting stars and lightning;
days of creation.

Has not this beauty lain dead among us for a thousand years?
Like maiden Snow-White sleeping in her glass coffin.
We have wandered over the ridge of her nose, we have trodden
       on her eyelids . . .

Now the mountains have risen up and begun to wander,
bearing the terrifying ball of the sun in their hands.
Our old eyes can see no more.
We cannot grumble. Praised be the hand
that hangs the wreath of stars on our ancient mountains.
As we perish we bless you, starry night beyond understanding.
Some time there will come a purer wind over the earth.
Then the human being will step out of mountains like these,
with the eternal light of greatness on its forehead.
Then Cosmos will be revealed. The riddles will fall echoing
into Minerva's immeasurable sacrificial bowl.'

— —

People, we shall forget ourselves
and be united with Cosmos again.
We shall hear the creator's voice
sound metallic out of the breast of things.
Nothing is enough for the longing that kneels
willing to draw a world to its breast.
Stream through us: eternal winds,
honey or heaven, blessing of the all!

— —

Let those who have heard and those who have seen
come to sacrifice on holy mountains.

Orpheus

I turn the snakes into angels.
Lift your heads! Stand on your tails!
One second . . . and they hiss no more.
Blissfully they lie at my feet,
dreaming, kissing my mantle's hem.
I touch my lyre. A wind goes over the earth
softly, solemnly, in tears
kissing beauty's lifeless, marble-white statues on the mouth
so that they open their eyes.
I am Orpheus. I can sing how I will.
All is pardoned me.
Tigers, panthers, pumas follow my steps
to my flat rock in the woods.

116

Hope

I want to be unconstrained –
therefore I care not a fig for noble styles.
I roll up my sleeves.
The poem's dough is rising . . .
Oh what a pity
that I cannot bake cathedrals . . .
Highness of forms –
goal of persistent longing.
Child of the present –
does your spirit not have a proper shell?
Before I die
I shall bake a cathedral.

[September 1918]

God Is Still Awake

What is wrong with me?
— The book is going to the publishers
— that makes everything clear.
The moon rises – my longing turns in. –
My longing turns and twists in bed
and laughs infernally:
God is still awake –
blessed sleepless angels round his throne!

[1918]

The Rose Altar (1919)

I.

The Rose Altar

I separate myself from you,
because I am more than you.

In dusk I am
a temple priestess
ordained watching over
the fire of the future.
————————————————————————————
I come out to you
with a joyous message:
the Kingdom of God is beginning.

Not Christ's
wasting empire,
but higher, brighter
human forms
come to the altar
bearing forth their gratitude
celestially scented,
overwhelming the senses.

There stands the altar –
like a sigh from God's breast –
crown it with roses
so that one only sees a mountain of beauty.
The moment's spirit
shall sit lightly thereon
drinking
the moment's skoal
out of fragile golden glass.

[September 1918]

The Road to Elysium and Hades

From the rock of destiny
you can clearly see how the road goes
to Elysium and Hades.

The people down there
wander in cloud-mist,
they weep and laugh,
follow coffins to graves
only in a dream.

Oh, how I long to be there,
where you can see
the road to Elysium and Hades.

First I want to climb Chimborazzo . . .

First I want to climb Chimborazzo
in my own country
and stand there breathlessly
with the wreath of victory.

Then I want to climb the mountain of fame,
to which the world's golden cornfields smile,
and stand there blessed
in rosy visions.

Last I shall climb the mountain of might,
as yet unclimbed,
from there the stars smile most gently
and give blessing to all.

In the Fairies' Hammock

Night and day
I lie in the fairies' hammock
and dream strange things.
That heart was not born to love me:
he will never cross the threshold of reality.
The lamp of Diana
shines through my nights
from beneath thin veils of fairy-tales.
I cannot love, I cannot abandon my great heart . . .
But one day I will lie down beside the finest son of the earth . . .
A little child
will drink at my breast of stone
the strongest milk of the earth.
I shall call him – Diana's gift.

My Artificial Flowers

My artificial flowers
I will send home to you.
My small bronze lions
I will set up by your door.
Myself I will sit down here on the stairway –
a lost pearl of the orient
in the big city's roaring sea.

The Storm

Now the earth shrouds itself once more in black. It is the storm
that rises from the night's abysses and dances
alone its ghostly dance over the earth.
Now people are fighting again – phantom against phantom.
What do they want, what do they know? They are driven
like cattle out of dark recesses,
they cannot tear themselves loose from the chain of events:
the great ideas drive their booty before them.
The ideas stretch out beseeching arms in the storm in vain,

he, the dancer, knows that he alone is master upon earth.
The world has no control over itself. One part of it will
collapse like a burning house, like a worm-eaten tree,
the other part will remain, protected by unknown hands.
And the sun watches all this, and the stars glow on ice-cold nights
and men steal furtively alone along the road to boundless
        happiness.

The Terrible Procession

Bravery is the highest, I say to you.
The angels of God are struggling with us,
the Kingdom of God stands on our strong side.
Unfold the red of your hearts
so one may see your glowing inscriptions.
the angels grasp hold of our banners.
What a procession, appalling, as if it were oneself being
        buried . . .
The dead walk with us, they grasp their wreaths,
they hurry.
Every terror, highest dread of progress
concentrated in a single breast!
One can only mourn at this procession
one's joy is too great.

On Foot I Had to Cross the Solar System

On foot
I had to cross the solar system
before I found the first thread of my red dress.
I sense myself already.
Somewhere in space hangs my heart,
shaking the void, from it stream sparks
into other intemperate hearts.

The Penitents

We shall do penance in the lonely forests.
We shall light solitary candles on the heaths.
We shall arise – one after the other.
When at last we look like one another as brothers and sisters
in strength and nobility –
then we shall go to the people.

[September 1918]

To the Strong

Flee into solitude! Be men!
Do not become dwarfs with shrunken limbs.
Do not become prisoners with clenched teeth.
Do not become eagles sick in chains and bonds.
Learn to stand like the fir trees on the rocks in the fire of
        the surf.
Learn to follow the unwritten laws of the stars.
Saints and heroes, pliant bodies, grow to pillars in truth's temple.
Learn how to rise like the waves in the storm.
Reach out your hands to your brothers, the world is becoming
        another.
The days of autumnal sorrow are forever past.

The Chalice of Suffering

Weaker hands may grasp the chalice of suffering
bringing it to paler lips,
my victor's lips avoid it yet.
But – no.
In my heart still sit giants with dark faces,
with stone hands pressed hard together.
One day they will come out of their dusks –
they will call to you – pain.
Come, sparking hammer, strike against the stone image.

124

Hew out my soul
that it may find words that never sat on human tongues.

The Earth Has Been Turned into an Ash-Heap

The earth has been turned into an ash-heap.
In penitent's clothes
I sit lightly on it and dream.
Oh how blissful are my dreams!
I am strong,
for I have risen up from death's marble bed.
Death – I looked you in the face, I held the scale towards you.
Death – your embrace is not cold, I myself am the fire.
Who is God? What has he done to us?
Do not blaspheme! He is near.
— — — — — — — — — — — — — — — — — —
From silver cups I pour pleasure over the earth
against which the dreams of Aphrodite grow pale.

My Fairy-Tale Castles

I looked into the philosopher's house*
and saw that he was happy . . .
But my fairy-tale castles
stand
on indescribable, fragile pillars.
Oh my fairy-tale castles,
collapse, collapse
into golden ruins.
I love you too much – die.

I shall build you up again
trembling
so as to kill you – you are too beautiful.
My fairy-tale castles
one day you will stand upon earth . . .
Then I will take away my hammer and chisel . . .
The world will have finished for me . . .

*Lichtenberg's shell

125

Where do the gods live . . .

Where do the gods live? In my heart,
in my ragged, painfully happy heart,
when the song arises.
Oh gods, what can a human being do in its few moments of life!
I have known your full might . . .

Gods, you come to me . . .
Afterwards I lie tired out and dream of you . . .
Oh gods, you visit me every day,
at the moment when I am full of might,
when my blood has gathered itself to hear your voices
you whisper words into my ears,
imperishable words like the diamonds on your toes.
Oh gods, gods!
In all my weakness I find mighty words –
words for you!
Is the world not ineffable,
since you have touched things with your enchanted hands?

No one has yet seen the world.
You hide it behind veils
— —
A ray of light has fallen on my poor path.

The Complaint of the Tool

Life sank back before me in blue smoke.
I stand high above all
with nothing above me but the threatening copper sky,
which I rule.
Why is this burden raised upon human shoulders?
Why has my heart been encased in iron armour?
Am I not permitted to be a human being?
The road lies, night black sorrow, behind me,
among rose coloured shadows I wander, a homeless god.
— —
Piece after piece you broke from my heart, too powerful god,

and made me to your instrument.
I belong to you, body and soul,
and with the remains of my forfeited life.
I weep. The tears fall where I go,
tears of one hard as stone.
Where can my mouth still find words to complain
of immobile superfluity?
My nights and days
are written in your book, O god.
Nothing belongs to me on earth,
not so much as a flower.
O to be the richest!
To have it written on one's forehead
that one must play the strange game of destiny
by necessity's command.

The Gods Are Coming

People do not know much about themselves,
they think themselves as poor as they seem to be in life,
they do not know that the gods live in their breasts
unrecognised.
The gods laugh. Life is theirs.
They drive the chariot with glowing harness.
In it sits a queen so magnificent
that the people only name her name in whispers.

Kneel down, people. The gods are coming.
The gods are rising up out of foreheads heavy with dust,
the gods are lifting the whole world to their height.

[1918]

Metamorphosis

What blessedness in the wind . . .
Kisses of eternity . . .
How my life has been metamorphosed and become still,
deceptively still . . .
Lucky fairy-tale princess,
your heart storms harder than the ocean's.
Does one carry in vain such a heart in one's breast?
Time, listen to my song!
When the damned sing like that in hell,
heaven's echo sometimes responds to them.
No my heart, you are going through the fire!
Can fate not terrify my godlike figure?
Do luck's tiny spirits not obey a wave of my hand?
Will the future not come if I call it?

[September 1918]

The Charm

How shall I speak to you out of my deepest heart?
How do the gods set down their words, irresistibly, lightly,
how shall I speak so that human weakness does not fell my
        words?
I want to speak so that I open the whole of my breast before you
and so that my will grips you with hard tongs
like a pain, fear, sickness, love . . .
I want you to grow weak from my will.
I want you to tear your hearts asunder
and demons to make their seat in your limbs
wild, inhuman, exploding all life.
Demons,
in all my earnest I want to look you in the eyes,
I will take all my being with me in my gaze.
Demons, longed-for: will I charm you forth with my power?
Mercilessly I throw my bait of golden locks before you.
My blood flows incessantly in thick streams.
Will you come one day to me, you vampires of the deep?

On the Steps of the Himalayas

On the steps of the Himalayas
great Vishnu sits
and dreams.

Endless is the evening around the Himalayas.

White-clad
the pilgrim stands small in the purple gleam.
Almighty,
take my life
for one moment of your dreams . . .
I want to see what it is you will – and perish . . .

The Song of the Ocean

Cautiously, cautiously,
what is it you press to your breast?
Do they look like you,
as these seas look like
the ocean weeping in fury?

Ocean, ocean,
you heave yourself from shore to shore
in unstilled longing,
you throb in the night
on the earth's iron rocks, so that they echo.

Ocean, ocean,
when your wrath subsides
you grow bright once more.
The new year's sun rises pale, but sure of victory, from your
    recesses.
The stiffened tongue of the waves sings of the roses' power
    the year round.

Question

I need nothing but God's mercy.
I go through life in a drunken stupor.
— — — — — — — — — — — — — — — — — — — —
O you strangely lightening reality — —
— — — is there an amphora
for my few drops of oil of roses?

The Torches

I want to light my torches above the earth.
My torch shall stand
in every nocturnal farm
of the alps, where the air is blessing,
in the tundras, where the sky is melancholy.
O my torch, light in the face of the terror-stricken,
the convulsed in tears, the darkened, the polluted.
A gentle god reaches out his hand to you:
without beauty no one can live for a second.

The Statue of Beauty

I saw beauty.
It was my destiny! Therein lies all.
How shall I say thank you?
Every day I strew fresh roses
plucked with hot hands
before your statue
so that your smile may rest on them.
Where shall I find roses
that do not shame my dreams?
This is my lot –
to go every day with roses to my queen
and lie sobbing at her feet . . .
When shall I rise up light as a feather
to fetch that rose, the only one, that never dies.

130

The Ring

In the eyes of the whole world
you must decide . . .
Will you enter the ring?
No one treads lightly into the ring.
The gods came to fetch you –
you stepped to one side,
it was not your time.
When the time comes
you will give the heart from your breast –
you will slowly grasp the hands in the ring.

The Martyr

The martyr is pale.
His eyes burn.
Compassionately he looks
down at you.

What do you know
who throng hither and thither
with beautiless movements,
of your good and bad,
how it feels to lift one's head freely.

He is acquitted
whom the whole world condemns.
Purest sun
is the black cup.

The motley cape of the victim
he takes lightly on his shoulders:
you stroke like velvet, like softest velvet –
the costume of my will.

II. – FANTASTIQUE

Spring Mystery

My sister
you come like a spring wind over our valleys . . .
The violets in the shadow breathe sweet fulfilment.
I will take you to the sweetest corner of the woods:
there we shall confess to each other how we saw God.

Letters from My Sister

Letters from my sister.
What can letters say
when I see you!
Does your hair not fall lightly round you in golden waves
when you come in
to tell me of your life?
Do the hems of your dress not stiffen in ecstasy as you walk?
          The earth carries you.
— — — — — — — — — — — — — — — — — — — —
Why does not everyone have eyes to see it,
why does a single hand scoop from the well of the gods?
Sister, my sister,
I have received your picture.

In the Darkness

I did not find love. I met no one.
Quaking I walked past Zarathustra's grave on autumn nights:
who hears me still on earth?
Then an arm was laid lightly around my life –
I found a sister . . .
I seize her by her golden locks –
is it you, the impossible?
Is it you?
Doubtfully I look into her face . . .
Is this how the gods play with us?

I Believe in My Sister

I go into the wilderness
and sit down alone on the rock,
the Devil's stone,
where sorrows have been waiting
for thousands of years.
I have a sister.
The elves wove her clothes of silk,
the moon-maiden sprinkled dew on her breasts . . .
She was beautiful – to arouse the passions of gods.

Oh this sister . . .
Were we not to tell stories to one another,
endless stories for a thousand years,
until eventually the dawn breaks –
our new dawn.

My sister . . .
Has she betrayed me?
Does she carry a dagger at her bosom – the light-footed
        one?
Answer me – laughing gaze.

No, no, a thousand times no! I do not believe it,
not even if the angels were to write it with indelible slate
          pencils on
the board of the ages . . .

Why did human weakness attack me?

I believe no one in the world but my sister . . .
What she says is true,
even if the world were to fall apart
my sister would never tell a lie.

All the Echoes in the Forest

No, no, no cry all the echoes in the forest:
I have no sister.
I go and lift up her white silk dress
and embrace it powerlessly.
I kiss you, I lay all my suffering upon you,
you thoughtless cloth!
Do you remember her rosy limbs?
Her shoes still stand in the sunshine,
the gods warm their hands at them.
Let snow fall over my sister's remains.
Let your bitter heart drive, snowstorm, over them.
With a shiver I shall tread that spot,
as the dreadful place where beauty was buried.

Sister

I once had a sister, a golden child.
In the city she vanished from me in the crowd.

When amidst black spruce trees I see
young birch trees shake their golden locks,
I remember my sister.

134

Is she standing wide-eyed amidst the trees
with beating heart,
is she stretching out her hands towards me?

Sister, my sister, where did they take you?
What dreams of pleasure can you dream
on beds of tiredness?

Child of heroes, child of luck!
We shall wait together
for the day of fairy-tales.

The Ineffable Is on its Way to Us

Who can love you, sister?
Is it not a dark-faced god who wants to enfold you in his arms?
Does he not stand at the foot of your bed while you fall asleep?
Shall our eyes see him, sister?
Did we not live in the fairy-tale, where the impossible is possible,
did I not say so sister?
Does the statue of beauty not mock us, around it the roses
        falling to dust?
Do these lips not promise all that there is upon earth?
Does this forehead not know that the ineffable is on its way to us?

The Child of God

The child of god sat with me.
The gold lyre sang out of my hands.
The child of god stares out into unending dusks.
The song circles over her head on broad wings.
What do you see in the song?
It is your own future that heaves itself
out of icy dusks,
your own bidding, calling, waiting future.

Sister, my sister . . .

Sister, my sister, you are only little,
but you have seen God,
blest is your brow, it shines so.
Since you saw God you have withdrawn from people.
You sat down alone among the trees
but the beck was silent for you,
the birds sang no more.
Whoever has seen God sees nothing more on earth,
he belongs at home in heaven.

III.

Dionysos

O Dionysos, you come with the horses of the sun out of
        distant space.
Swollen with weeping, the earth waits, a woman at prayer.
O Dionysos, Dionysos!
above our heads we hear the thunder of your horses.
Liberation, liberation
sing the swift reins.
O Dionysos, Dionysos,
I clamber up onto your horses,
with mad hands I hold fast to the chariot's wheels.
The mad can do anything.
A ray of spring sunshine, I climb down into your chariot.
Around us nothing but spring-blue space.
When choirs of birds exult on earth
your horses gallop like the storm.
All spaces sing the resurrection.

Fragments of a Mood

I

Wind, wind, wind!
Strew roses and narcissi from the garden of my memories,
where my young dreams wander.
The wall of the mountains stands high,
upland sun glows wildly in my hair.
Empty garden, will you give no answer?
— — — — — — — — — — — — — — — — — —
I and he that is dead belong together.
The bitter narcissi's taste on my tongue
repeats: farewell, farewell, farewell, farewell . . .
I fill my fist with ashes from his urn
and hold it to the sky: What have I here?
White clouds, lay yourselves over light-blue abysses:
witness, witness
that he is ashes who was the light of the sun.

II

My wild longing looks at you.
So the upland summer looks from the forest.
How can a son of the upland die?
Now summer is coming again over the meadows.
Caltha palustris drinks from the foam of the beck.
The ravines are full of mist.
The upland gods play their melancholy pipes.
The one who understood their song has gone.
He, whose soul was melancholy as the light that wanders
          over the heights,
has long since gone far away over mountain and sea.

I love the mountains, the love of my youth lies in them.
Over tender, green crocuses, over my first budding love
strides remembrance with triumphant feet.
So one might drag unwillingly with one a young
captive barbarian with lightning yellow locks.

138

Was I not young with lightning yellow locks then –
— —
— —
— —
— —

It sometimes happens when the rose-bush flowers
that the thorns' dry tangle is strewn with rosy miracles.
This is what happened to me, too — — — — —— — — — —
— —
My memories flame up like the fires of retreating soldiers
over ravaged stretches of land,
as the marshes in the north are covered with white flowers
          in spring,
as *fata morgana* raises its dumb processional flag
before the converted, believing, delirious wanderer.
When does one see such things? When life wants to prove
          its might.
When it rises up on its boldest mountain peak
in order to pray in vertigo.

The Hour of Sacrifice

Hear the clock strike.
It is the hour of sacrifice.
The clock strikes.
What have you left to sacrifice?
You have been lying on the sacrificial altar
for many years.
To lay oneself down there
is no pain.
Whom else will you sacrifice?
You still love, you still love,
say no more.

You gave away the whole world,
you learned to walk on heavenly roads.
In your hand the rose is dead,
the wind does not touch your cheek.
Whom else will you sacrifice?
When the hour strikes
you shall answer this question:
then you will make your choice
with life and death as witnesses.

Scherzo

Up there stars, unambiguously clear, on earth my heart, the
      unambiguously clear.
Magnificent night of stars, we are one.
Do I not sit trembling on a rope of stars . . . as if it might break?
Time, is it you, sleepy abyss, that yearningly mocks me?
Danger for wearying dancers' feet,
danger for weakening climbers' arms,
danger for the daringly stretched rope of pearls.

Time – perish!
Every star blinks me in the face: I am you!
Every star kisses me on the mouth: stay with me!
The stars close a ring around me, closer, closer,
the whole of my upper body enters a mist of stars.
What shall I do in there? Shall I weep?
The evening dreams. The sea-king drinks a skoal from a
      mussel shell.
No one will move. But the dancing girl, let her rise
forth on midnight toes
and fall on her knees and stretch out her arms
and kiss the beautiful one.

Roses

The world is mine.
Wherever I go
I throw roses at everyone.
The artist loves every marble ear that hears his words.
What are pain, misery to me?
Everything has fallen with a crash:
I sing.
So rises pain's great hymn out of a happy breast.

POEMS OF 1919-20 FROM
The Land That Is Not

Captivity

Captive, captive . . . I want to cut my fetters.
I go through life with painfully angry lips.
My abysses, why do I enquire into you, you deserve no name.
Bronze joins itself to bronze and becomes a human being,
and the human being has iron in its heart.
But does the bronze really have this frightening gleam on its
      brow
from the god of the lightnings?
I throw my heart on the roadway, let the vultures devour it –
the full moon will bear me a new one.

[February 1919]

Pale-Hearted Night

Pale-hearted night, you are listening . . .
No, that is not true, half of your blood is powerful enough.
When it rises in your veins
and goes to battle, the world is yours.

Pale-hearted night, when your blood is up, forward and going
      to battle,
your veins are then an empty fortress,
dismally abandoned,
while the battle rages for the iron gates.
An abandoned castle rules the world,
the nameless castle of power.
One day your dark blood will return singing.

My Life, My Death and My Destiny

I am nothing but a boundless will,
a boundless will, but for what, for what?
All things are dark around me,
I cannot lift a straw.
My will wants only one thing, but it is a thing I do not know.
When my will breaks loose, I shall die.
Welcome, my life, my death and my destiny.

Motley Observations (1919)

The houses we actually live in are prehistoric huts in comparison with the conception of a human dwelling which we carry within us.

One should not say: the universe, for how is it possible to gather into one concept what cannot be measured?

Free will is an absurd hypothesis, something independently operating of its own accord in an abstract thought-space.

A great form-creating imagination is an unredeemed spirit if it is not discharged in painting.

The final and highest refinement of vanity is the destruction of all vanity, just as a woman can be sure of playing most safely with a man whom she does not need.

Freedom from prejudice is sureness in dealing with things.

There is something unappetizing about laying hands on one's own life.

The good person should be able to neutralize the harmful effects of his behaviour through severity.

It is one of the most difficult things in this world of unclear concepts to fight within oneself what one does not carry within oneself.

Evil persons are most often powerful organisms that feel hemmed in by the flood of their own temperament. That the evil suffer most is not true, their suffering is not deep, in one sense it is a pleasant habit for them.

A high degree of intelligence lends the face something rich and mellow, it is as if the fat of the spirit had risen into the face. Minerva's fat.

Now commonplace people are hanging the bell of patriotism around their necks as if it were theirs.

Gösta Berling can present himself even to a very spoilt reader, who gives him from his own inner self the most exquisite seasoning: then a centaur is created.

Men of great success are realists and fatalists.

The task of the improver of mankind is not to preach morality, but to alter the inner self of mankind by transforming the external conditions for its moral health.

Morality has begun where it should end, i.e. by giving a clue to those who long for self-perfection.

Hitherto everything has happened to individuals, the religions have appeared in their deeper meaning to individuals, but now we can discern a time when the masses will be the object of cultivation.

Ordinary people are quite sensual in their own way, a contented way that great temperaments cannot tolerate.

Misunderstanding has hitherto been the greatest power on earth.

The highest degree of genius is the most accommodating and the least accommodating.

All long roots of truth are suspect, we only get the truth out in short, broken bits.

Our weakness in defending or attacking lies always in our fear of failure, which makes us use force when it is enough for us merely to throw in some annihilating suspicions with a careless hand.

We never surrender our innermost arch-superstition – that would be our ruin.

People have not sufficient character to forbid publicly the highest utterances of the human spirit. Scholars, journalists, etc. are detours rendering everything innocuous.

We see first what is coarsest about truth, i.e. truth itself. The most important thing, the person who tells it, is seen only much later.

That life surrounds us and we have no time for it sharpens its fascination in a subtle way, just as Heaven intensifies the earth's fascination for the religious.

The emptiness of life, which appears to people of today as monasticism, has provoked a hysterical passion for amusement, the flesh which believes itself to be oppressed is taking its rightful due. It might amuse a Mephistopheles to lead this headlessly scurrying mass out onto slippery ice – to offer it once the full cup of enjoyment.

If men of genius with puritanical blinkers happen to see the truth, they become unbelievably inventive about explaining it away.

A non-religious nature always has a slight sympathy with Mephistopheles where the singing of the angels is concerned.

Through misunderstanding religion can become a source of anti-culture when religions make themselves deaf to worldly art and science and thus avoid the influences of genius they are in need of.

It is so strange about the art of aphorism: the play with contrasts is as trivial as a word-play, the truths are most often unremarkable, and yet this is the costume of truth, more priceless than anything else, that is being woven.

To say that one loves mankind is hysteria, to say that one does not love it is weakness – there is only one right way: to have the power to make it into what it ought to be.

The person who is not yet mild himself longs all the more intensely for the triumph of mildness, as for a cause the victory of which is uncertain and which has many enemies within himself.

Ordinary people are naive and literal in their virtues, perhaps because these are so new to them.

A thinker of greater genius than there has been hitherto would need fewer words than the philosophers have used until now. In the future the work which has to be done will be harder and quantitatively less.

The proletariat's extravagance is poorly grown life-energy. The proletariat is an atom of growth which the earth asks: why are you still sucking at me? The earth loves plants that suck with deep roots.

There is one thing we always have before others: ourselves.

No one has any control over his star. One is *forced* to follow it.

One has always been worthy of the partner one receives in one's marriage.

If one wants mankind to attain to something high, it is better somewhat to overvalue than to undervalue it.

The sleepwalker walks to the lottery to draw the great lot.

When one's own intellect has risen high, every intellect appears worthy of attention, irrespective of whether it is that of a man or of an insect, one's eyes are opened to the demonic in the intellect's inner essence.

The truly vile comes to meet one when something high is thrown in the mire. In a similar context it once came to meet me: in a dream I saw evil hags mockingly drown little children in pails, I saw executions everywhere on shores and hills, human hands and branches of trees sullied with blood and brains, all so crude and vile that it could not exist in reality, only in the magnifying mirror of a monstrously insulted sensibility.

Mild insomnia intensifies genius.

Conscious virtue, the virtue that merits talking about, begins only with the education of the intellect, before that everything is animal chance.

Thinkers join together the great stones in thought's edifice, amateurs are the mortar which can be dispensed with in a building that is simply thought together.

The truly declassed and outcast among men are only those who have committed a base deed.

A real art-critic would be a person who could grasp the inner unity of law among the different art-forms, art-characters.

The highest things that are visible to us lie on the other side of good and evil, vile and beautiful, and there the highest things created by the human spirit become small, narrow and all-too-human, there objects speak, the art of the future becomes cosmic.

Nietzsche's strength is not to be sought in the strength of his voice, but in the highness that streams from his greatest experience – the eternal return.

Should not every great human being above all else have his own great destiny, an individual focus in life?

The reviewer is often someone who speaks at such length about a book that at last no one knows what its worth is any longer. If criticism is to fulfil its aims, critics should expressly declare, beyond any shadow of a doubt, what a book is. Books need their trade-mark just like other wares.

Guilt-feelings are always a sure sign of weakness of character, true guilt remains a question-mark.

Most people perish because they chase after that which glitters and miss what is really necessary. We are all like magpies and pikes, we grasp after that which glitters – in our own minds.

When the spirit is oppressed the flesh groans.

It is necessary to learn to pack one's intellectual kitbag in order to see how elegant, well-ordered and light to carry one's luggage is.

Woman's greatest merit is that until now she has not greatly sinned intellectually.

Danger and insecurity are the true element of nonchalance, civilized life is hard to tolerate.

There comes a time when one says to oneself: my thoughts no longer belong to me – and then one dedicates all of one's life to others.

There are persons to whom everything eventually comes, and others who have the privilege of going to everything themselves.

Life's three greatest gifts: poverty, loneliness, suffering are treasured only by the wise man at their true value.

Is there anything more seductive than Napoleon's brazen, godlike adventurer's mug?

A real man needs no name, he comes, sees and conquers.

What we need now is the most brazen man, the one who once bore the name of Napoleon.

Those who are not men of action say that the masses smell bad, but Napoleon has no nose and the waves carry him.

Every time a sense of constriction comes over one, one should transform it into a sense of expansiveness.

Where beauty is lacking all the graces take one another by the hand and flee. Then instead of love comes righteousness, and duty instead of regal inclination.

Whoever has power over hearts should treat them as something holy.

A great inborn external chic, which is as rare as great physical beauty, is accompanied by an inner stylishness, an exquisiteness in every act and gesture. These persons know themselves to be rulers and are recognised as such by others.

A humanity as pure as flowers is the ideal of the future.

Poems about the cosmos could only be whispers.

It is not necessary to pray, one looks at the stars and has the feeling of wanting to sink down to the ground in wordless adoration.

One should not ask if God exists or does not exist, one should lay one's small intelligence aside.

The prejudice against God is the hardest to overcome.

154

The Shadow of the Future (1920)

THE PLANETS ARE RISING

The Mystery

All people are playthings.
Yesterday I was a plaything myself.
Today I am the one who reveals the mystery.
I want everyone to come to me,
I want everyone to hear the beating of my heart.
Fire and blood and the chrism of the future you shall take
      from my hands.
I want to baptise the whole of mankind into the future.
I shall convert everyone to a more sacred god.
I want to sweep out all superstition with a soundless broom,
jeering I want to kill all pettiness.
I want to tread on your great serpent; I want to split his
      head with my sword.
O you my good sword, that I have received from Heaven, I
      kiss you.
You shall not rest
until the earth is a garden where gods dream over miraculous
      cups.

Tolerance

Can you catch in your hands a star that is rising towards the zenith,
can you measure its flight?
Do not hinder it from rising.
A glow of planets falls upon earth, foreign to your hand.
Strange and hot is the glow of the planets to a foreign hand.
Let the planets rise. Star after star.
A hot longing comes over the earth:
a star with a redder gleam than the others shoots forth: out of
     the way.
A hand that follows its own law wants to upturn that which others
     fortify.
A victor is coming, inaudible lips pronounce the coercer's name.

Might

I am the commanding strength. Where are those who will
     follow me?
Even the greatest bear their shields like dreamers.
Is there no one who can read the power of ecstasy in my eyes?
Is there no one who can understand when in a low voice I say
     light words to those nearest?
I follow no law. I am a law unto myself.
I am the person who takes.

An Old Ruler

Earth, on your back I have raised a castle for conquerors,
the powerfully laden shall be guests in it,
the powerfully laden who walk and wait.
There stand melancholy windows,
speaking of shattered destinies,
there you shall wander young, you untrembling
people of bronze like me.

And your breasts shall sing like a spring storm
whipping the window-pane with wet wings.
Blessed, laughing you will seize a new star in your hands,
then your features will grow dark, your gaze will fall earthwards.
What power this arm lays into the sword,
which shall pierce through — — — — — — — — — — — —
— —
— —

Young breast . . . why is it so light in you?

Hostile Stars

Hostile stars are rising.
Eternally foreign, eternally far
you seek to smile at each other, betrayed by human trust.
Each star has a gaze of ice.
Each star is proud and alone in its power
and has no faith in the glitter of stars.
Each star wants to make you believe it is all.
Each star is blessed like nothing else in the world.
Each star want to set the world on fire with its blazing points.
Each star advances like a red glow in the distance
to destroy, to devour, to burn, to exercise its power.

Creator Forms

My heart of iron wants to sing its song.
To compel, compel
the sea of humans,
to form, to form
the great mass of humans
so as to delight the gods.
Swaying in loose saddles we are coming,
we the unknown, nonchalant, strong.
Does the wind carry us?
Like a mocking laugh sound our voices from afar, afar . . .

Wallenstein Profile

Approaching night, I play catch with you,
– my gruesome dice.
My hand is heavy and unafraid, with evil powers
it plays its game, they never refuse to help.
My dice falls heavy with destiny.
Hail, the path of might goes through the underworld.
Through the narrowest cliff-paths of the underworld goes he
      that seeks the wreath that does not fade.

The Stars Are Teeming

The stars are rising! The stars are teeming! Strange evening.
A thousand hands lift the veil from the face of the new age.
The new age looks down upon the earth: a melting hot gaze.
Madness flows slowly into human hearts.
Golden folly grips human thresholds with the passion of
      heavy creepers.
Human beings open their windows to a new longing.
Human beings forget everything on earth to listen to a voice
      that is singing far above them:
Each star throws its farthing to earth with a bold hand:
      ringing coins.
From each star comes a plague on creation:
the new sickness, the great happiness.

The Planets

Wild earth that rolls onward into burning, cutting space,
blissful that the air rasps against your cheek,
blissful that the journey spins you round.
Planets want nothing else than the swiftness of their paths.
Shores of the universe twinkle like questions.
Swifter, harder, more mercilessly, weltering in miraculous
      destinies,
the countless hordes of the planets roll by
towards a light gleam in the west –
possibility's single staked-out way.

THE SHADOW OF THE FUTURE

The Shadow of the Future

I sense the shadow of death.
I know that our destinies lie piled high on the Norns' table.
I know that not a drop of rain is absorbed by the earth
that is not written in the book of the eternal ages.
I know as certainly as the sun will rise
that I shall never see the endless moment when it stands at
      its zenith.

The future casts its blessed shadow on me;
it is nothing else than flowing sun:
pierced through with light I shall die,
when I have crushed all chance with my foot I shall turn
      smilingly away from life.

Thou Great Eros

Thou great Eros. Thou breathest weddings.
But what kind of weddings?
Since the earth has been, and desire married two bodies,
the lightning-bolt has not neared
human brows.
This lightning-bolt strikes,
this lightning-bolt is all powerful,
the lightning-bolt does with human children what it will.

160

What Is My Homeland?

What is my homeland? Is it far-off, star-strewn Finland?
No matter what it is. Low stones, roll on flat shores.
I stand on your grey granite as on a certainty.
Thou certainty, thou shalt always strew laurel and roses in
      my path.
I am the deity that approaches with victorious brow.
I am the blessed conqueror of the past.

Bliss

Soon I will stretch myself on my bed,
small spirits shall cover me with white veils
and they shall strew red roses on my bier.
I am dying – for I am too happy.
I will even clench my teeth in bliss around my shroud.
I will curl my feet with bliss inside my white shoes,
and when my heart stops voluptuousness will lull it to sleep.
Let my bier be taken to the market-place –
here lies the bliss of earth.

Tantalus, Fill Your Beaker

Are these poems? No, these are shreds, scraps,
workaday slips of paper.
Tantalus, fill your beaker.
Impossibility, impossibility,
dying I shall one day throw the garland from my locks into
      your eternal emptiness.

F

The Lost Crown

I grieve as though I had lost a fairy-tale crown.
O crown of every dream,
must this pale forehead incline, resign itself?
I have found everything.
Must I deny the victor, teach him humility?

The Temple of Eros

I saw that the temple of Eros was made of human bodies.
Inside, the god's image, eternally the same.
What his lips offer, no one has understood,
what he thinks about most inwardly, no one knows.
His glances merely lash the carelessly young bodies,
which play with one another.
We do not know his pleasure — — — — — — — — — — — —
— —
We playmates of Eros, we want only one thing:
to be fire of your fire and to burn up.

The Sun

I stand as on clouds in a bliss without likeness.
The edges of the clouds burn red. It is the sun.
The sun has kissed me. Like it kisses nothing upon earth.
Am I to live eternally as a witness of this moment?
Alas, no, I am to climb up the vertical rays
nearer her.
One day
I shall spin myself into the sun like a fly into amber,
it will be no jewel for those who come after me,
but I have been in the glowing oven of bliss.
Woe, you crown that gleams on my forehead,
what will they know when they see you?

162

The Net

I have the net into which all fishes go.
Blissfully the fisherwoman's quiet breast heaves
when she draws the silver load to herself.
I lift up the riches of the earth on my shoulders.
I bear you, I bear you to a fairy-tale pond.
Upon the shore stands a fisherman with golden fishing rods.
There are gods somewhere behind the densest forests,
we wandering human children want to go nowhere but there.
Up to seek the burning sun of the future beyond the forest.

Resurrection Mystery
(occasional poem)

Heaven's angels sing down to earth: tear apart the veil of
    death, tear it down!

A woman lies bedded in a black room.
Great candles burn round her bier.
In her face there is a desire for Life,
as if her hands would like to clasp themselves in prayer.
It is silent, only night walks round with watching steps.
Suddenly a fire flames red above the dead one: what is this?
It is silent in the room.
Angels sing: black walls, grow wide!
In the light of blue heaven must the coffin stand blessed.
The coffin stands in eternity's room.
Angels sing: thou child of God, the Lord is calling thee.
It is silent, never shall sorrow leave this dwelling.
But the dead one hears the call:
Yes, Lord, I come, sounds her voice like an echo through all
    heavens.

THE ELF-QUEEN'S SCEPTRE
AND OTHER POEMS

The Elf-Queen's Sceptre
(Fragment)

Where is he,
the one I saw in a dream of ecstasy?
Where is he,
the one my helpless arms never reach?
Where is he,
the one the shadow on my forehead denies?
Where is he,
that lifts a tired flower from the road
and wraps her in transparent silk
and winds the veils around her feet
and looks at her wondering long: how did you die, child?
My pale face will not change colour,
on my forehead stands written in heavy letters: she sleeps.
Your tears shall fall down on my feet,
they shall trickle between my knees,
as if they would wake me to life.
My loneliness
cries loudly out of an empty coffin.
It is as if something wanted to sit up with clasped hands
and has not the strength to do it.
And you shall lift up my coffin on two pillars in your
        wonderful garden.
And you shall order the golden locks on my forehead
and stroke into place the silk on my belly.
Your hand shall be wet with tears
and you shall say: here I still pluck
my wonderful fruits, fragile and frozen.
And you shall pluck the purest roses in your garden.

Is this one pure enough?
You lay it in my hand
which holds it trustingly as if it were living and warm.
And you lay a thin green leaf on my bare breast
so that I may lean my chin on it as on a psalter.
From one side you playfully hold up
my silken-soft locks with your hand
and lay them back on the white silk cushion.
My ear is as if it were listening to silver sounds out of strained
    distance.
With a silver powder-puff you touch my glowing lips, behind
    which the teeth show white.
And you think: are you not alive?
Then you lift me up with both arms and lay me down in the
    grass
and you sit and look at me with waking eyes, as a mother
    looks at her child.
You take my limp hand and draw the diamond ring from my
    finger,
you bore the stone into the flesh of my upper arm.
Through red veils you see that I am alive.
And you unfasten my dress
and lay your hand on my heart to listen.
You undress me,
the silk falls down my shoulders.
You take and lay my wonderful head against your breast as
    for a kiss,
but it falls back lifelessly.
Yet you have more courage, you take my fingers
and bend them back at the joints, as if they belonged to a
    child.
Then a blue tower shall rise up in your garden.
The elves dance round it.
Up in the golden pinnacles the elf-queen walks to and fro.
To the elf-queen, the elf-queen! the cry comes from your breast.
Elf-queen, elf-queen, answer me in broad daylight.
— —
The elf queen's voice is a flute: girls, hurry.
The elves hurry from all directions.
On the foot of the coffin they spread a golden gauze,
on the sides of the coffin they sit
and a little elf has fallen asleep on the silver cushion.

They station themselves on the brown feet of the betrothed
they sit on his head amidst his brown hair,
on the bride the elves climb as on a rock.
                    He turns away: what avails it me
that the elves comb her golden hair,
that they lay silver poppies on her breast?
I let the ring fall back with a chime into the coffin.
Are you mad? cried a little elf and drew a hair from his head.
Observe the faithlessness of men!
And the elves all rushed up over him,
that he stood there like a white ghost.
Highest up on top stood the elf-queen with a glittering crown
                    and raised her sceptre:
inside the black alder lives the cat Elektrus,
ask him to come hither to purr the dead one to life
— —
'Is my flower alive? The ring in my hand has seen all sorrow.
Happily I place it again on my finger, your wonderful plaything.
Plaything of playthings, you set your white shoes upon the
                    earth again.
When the moon rises behind the great spruce tree
we shall hurry, blissfully pressed close to one another
out into the dark wood.
Then I shall hold you in my arms
like a promise of an even stiller day.'
'Then I shall kiss you on the forehead, great-eyed saviour.
The forest is full of violets,
darkly the spring-water hastens forth, mumbling thanks.
This ring shall gleam forever on my finger like a memory.
                    Could we still die?
It is hard to believe it. Life floats with violet-coloured waves.
One cannot believe that the lightning can strike down a
                    thick tree
with titanic din.'

The Waterfall

Creator's anguish round my heart,
clouds around me which I kiss with my mouth.
Clouds, do you know what will become of me?

166

I will go today to see a fortune-teller.
Raise your hand and show me my future.
I see your two eyes like steel.

O thundering waterfall of pleasure.
the foam that purls on your bank makes a mind mad.
Thundering, hurtling fall, you need ask nothing.
Eternally the same certainty turns thousandfold somersaults.
Melancholy certainty: that you are irresistible and superfluous.

Eros' Secret

I live red. I live my blood.
I have not denied Eros.
My red lips burn on your cold sacrificial slabs.
I know you, Eros –
you are not man and woman,
you are the power
that sits crouched in the temple,
before, raising itself, wilder than a scream,
more violently than a slung stone,
slinging out the apt words of the annunciation over the world
from the temple door of the almighty.

Eros Is Creating the World Anew

Eros is creating the world anew.
The soil in his hands is full of wonders.
Eros does not see men's petty squabbles,
he sees with his burning gaze
how suns and moons complete their orbits.
They are so near his pregnant soul,
what is it that his wild mind dreams?
The stars course singing along their orbits
but on Eros' forehead an eternal miracle is already dawning.
The young giant senses already the great blind saga
that he plays once more.

Lightning

Lightning swathed in clouds,
blue lightning that I see,
when will you break forth?
Lightning, you blessed one,
laden with thunder, fearsome, purifying,
I wait exhaustedly for you.
My body lies like a rag
so as one day, grasped by electric hands,
firmer than all the ore of the earth,
to emit lightning.

Instinct

My body is a mystery.
So long as this fragile thing lives
you shall feel its might.
I will save the world.
Therefore Eros' blood hurries to my lips,
and Eros' gold into my tired locks.
I need only look,
tired or downcast: the earth is mine.

When I lie wearily on my bed
I know: in this weary hand is the world's destiny.
It is the power that quivers in my shoes,
it is the power that moves in the folds of my garments,
it is the power that stands before you –
there is no abyss for it.

Solitude

There are so few among the sand of the sea who understand it.
Alone I came, alone I must go.
My free heart has no brother.
Christian ghosts sit in every heart and stretch out poverty's
    hands.
That sweetness that streams to me from every side is
    inaccessible to you.
It is the wonderful solitude of the throne,
it is wealth, the wealth that makes knees bend.

The Strong Man's Body

I know, I know that I shall win the victory.
Whatever men may call me, whosoever may await me, I am
    the star of the future.
I have awoken on a primordial throne,
wonderful hands spread silken veils beneath me.
The mystery passes in my veins.
Mystery, I recognise you, I, the anti-mystic, enemy of ghosts.
Mysteries have no clear boundaries, mysteries have no
    outspoken name,
the mystery surges in the strong man's body when
    drunk-blind he goes to action.

Premonition

O you most glorious of all that is glorious, my body,
how is it you know that you have power?
This arm is what the century has need of.
The lightning sits in my hand and one day it will flash forth,
men will see its blue gleam and comprehend.
I am only one among others and others are stronger than I,
but I am the shield people shall look to,
I am the kernel and the link that connects.

At Sunrise

People, people,
as the rain falls down from heaven
I step down to earth.

My blessed eyes have seen the stars,
I caught the lightning in my right hand,
power, power floods over my lips.

Destiny set me on watch over the rising sun.
Hailed be the expanses around us –
a new day is coming in.

O you my heart's expanse . . .

O let me spread out my arms, life.
O you my heart's expanse. I wait
to hear my voice.
I want to speak, my words shall fall like glowing firebrands
      among the crowd.
———————————————————————
There is no hand to touch the surface of my heart and make
      it tremble
yet I seem to gather the girdle of the thunders round my
      breast.
But the thunder is in my breast, it shall fall like a shot.
I am a god in whom storms rage,
with sucking eyes I draw all into my soul.

Materialism

In order not to die I have to be the will to power.
In order to avoid the atoms' struggle in their break-up.
I am a chemical mass. I know so well,
I do not believe in seeming and soul,
the game of games is so foreign to me.

Game of games, I play you and believe not for one moment.
Game of games, you taste good, you breathe a wonderful scent,
yet there is no soul and there has never been any soul.
It is seeming, seeming, seeming, and sheer play.

Ecstasy

It is dangerous to desire when one is the powerful one,
therefore my desires stand still.
———————————————————————
Woe, the past is dreaming,
woe, we hold the unopened bowls of tomorrow in our hands,
woe, purest of all that is pure,
woe, bliss that lifts the hammer to destroy,
woe, bliss that sleeps in the breast of tomorrow.
Pleasure that becomes pain,
bliss that one only looks at with tears in one's eyes and that
        dies away.
With tears in the corners of my eyes I pronounce the words
        of bliss over the doomed world.
Why doomed? Because you cannot hear the voices of bliss,
because you sleep like a foetus in its mother's womb.

Bliss brushed against this brow that names itself mortal,
through my lips streams the heat of a god,
all my atoms are separate and on fire . . .

Hamlet

What does my mortal heart want? My mortal heart is silent.
        My mortal heart wants nothing.
Here lies the whole earth. You turn away in cramp.
A magic wand has brushed against this earth and it has
        become dust.
And there I sit upon ruins,
I know that you are coming, unforeseen hour.

I know that you are waiting behind a bolted door,
that I can approach you and you cannot reach me with your
    hand.
There is no choice for me,
truth, I will follow you if you go into the land of mists.
Truth, truth, do you dwell in mortuaries among worms and
    dust?
Truth, do you dwell there where is everything I hate?
Truth, do sorrowful lanterns light your way?

The Hyacinth

I

I stand so brave, so expectant and blissful.
Shall destiny pelt me with snowballs?
Let the snow run in my brown hair,
let the snow cool my blessed throat.
I raise my head. I have my secret. What is there with power
    over me?
I am unbroken, a hyacinth that cannot die.
I am a spring flower with pure bells
that rises full of the field's carefree triumph:
to live unsurpassably, securely, without opposition in the world.

II

I grow up a hyacinth from iron hard ground.
Break me with your powerful, sap-filled hands – Life.
I kiss your hand which is more full of sap than I.
Break me to make an adornment for a queen.
If there is a carefree and untroubled queen,
let her hold the hyacinth like a sceptre in her hand,
the spring's pure symbol, kindred to the sun.

Four Little Poems

I

How can there be such bliss in a breast?
is the only question in my philosophy.
And my only answer is: because, because I know.
What is it I know?
That I shall be swooned in sun
and not be dead and not victorious,
a sun that cannot bear its own rising.

II

My crown is too heavy for my strength.
Look, I can lift it up with ease,
but my remains will fall apart.
My remains, my remains, you are wonderfully bound together.
My remains, I believe you are beginning to long for a coffin.
Now it is not the electric hour,
my remains, you do not belong to me.

III

I am triumphant as life itself.
Do my hands not bring luck?
Strange time, you foster heroes' children with untouched locks
on heights where no hands reach.
And again my heart stands over abysses and triumphs.
My heart, how carefree you are,
as if these were so many pebbles to play with!

IV

It rains, it rains on me in violent streams.
— — — — — — — — — — — — — — — — — — —
For so little I will not yet sunder my heart.
Let misfortunes blow like cold winds round me.
I am prosperity itself. On my forehead stands written:
'The sun cannot weep for one moment.' Whosoever wants to
        kill the sun must surrender,
he will see who is strongest.

Animal Hymn

The red sun rises
without thoughts
and is alike to all.
We rejoice at the sun like children.
There will come a day when our remains will fall apart,
it is all the same when it happens.
Now the sun shines into the inmost recesses of our hearts
filling all with absence of thought
strong as the forest, the winter and the sea.

Sun

I am blissful.
Reckless morning sun, shine into my face, brush against my
        forehead.
No, you hear already the answer of my proud heart.
My heart becomes more arrogant with each revolution of
        the sun.
It is as if I held the sun's disc in my hands,
merely so as to crush it.
It is as if I were a guest on earth by chance, in passing, lightly
so as to waken it with a shower of derisive words.
O you most arrogant of hearts, stretch out your arms towards
        the sun,
fall on your knees and let your breast be pierced through by
        the sun, the sun.

Resolve

I am a very mature person,
but no one knows me.
My friends have a false picture of me.
I am not tame.
I have weighed tameness in my eagle's claws and know it well.
O eagle, what sweetness in the flight of your wings.

174

Will you be silent like everything else?
Will you write poetry perhaps? You shall write no more poetry.
Every poem shall be the tearing-up of a poem,
not a poem but clawmarks.

The Lightning's Yearning

I am an eagle.
That is my confession.
Not a poet,
never anything other.
I despise everything other.
For me there is nothing other than to wheel in eagle's flight.
What occurs in eagle's flight?
Always the same, the eternal.
A lightning shoots down on the sky in endless eagerness
full of secret love as when a new world is born.

The Great Garden

We are all homeless wanderers
and we are all brothers and sisters.
Naked we go in rags with our knapsacks,
but what do princes possess in comparison with us?
Treasures stream to us through the air,
they cannot be measured by the weight of gold.
The older we grow
the more surely we know that we are brothers and sisters.
We have nothing else to do with the rest of creation
than to give it our souls.
If I had a great garden
I would invite all my brothers and sisters to it.
Each and every one would take with him a great treasure.
Since we have no homeland we could become a people.
We would build a trellis around our garden
so that no sound from the world could reach us.
From our silent garden
we would give the world a new life.

The Star

What do you know? What do you know?
It is dangerous to say.
I feel luck in my hand, luck itself,
I have luck, great luck, in my fingers.

O miraculous luck!
I belong to those who believe in their star:
that is to grasp the secret forces of destiny.
What can the secret forces of destiny do when one grasps them
with hands strong with truth?

Harmful words, harmful.
But my star will never deny itself.
In the face of my star that threatening stands
I feel my inadequacy.
Where will I find the heavy hand that grasps the sword?
Do not ask me, says my star,
human child, cover your face before that which cannot be
        grasped,
that which is your own, your own will give you strength.

Thoughts about Nature

We see life and death with our eyes, they are sun and moon.

So through the universe course the life-giving suns, the destroying moons, the planets submitting themselves to life and death.

Around all that is sick the moon spins its net, until the full moon comes to fetch it one beautiful night.

Dying children of nature love death, they long for the moment when the moon will take them.

Nature is intimate with death, it experiences death every night. It submits itself with equal willingness to the sorcery of the sun or of the moon.

Death is a sweet poison – decay, but there is nothing unhealthy about death. Nature is health itself and sees that death is just as healthy as life.

In decay lies the highest beauty and the devil is God's highest goodness. Wonderful is the swift work of destruction in autumn.

Nature stands under God's protection. The devil has no power over nature. Nature is God's darling.

If we do not become children of nature we cannot reach the kingdom of Heaven, for the religious mysteries are the mysteries of nature. They throve not in the temples of Judaea, but in the ignorant child of nature who felt with the lilies of Sharon.

Nature's path to God is direct, eternal and objective, without external chance.

The human heart that seeks God has to struggle against subjectivity, for the heart begins on the other side of subjectivity. But the path of nature is protected.

[September 1922]

LAST POEMS FROM
The Land That Is Not

The Gypsy Woman

I am a gypsy woman from a foreign land,
I hold the cards in brown hands full of secrets.
Days follow after days, monotonous and motley.
Defiantly I look people in the face:
how can they know that the cards burn?
How can they know that the pictures live?
How can they know that each card is a destiny?
How can they know that each card that falls from my hand
has a thousandfold meaning?

No one knows that these hands seek something.
No one knows that these hands were sent out long ago.
That these hands are familiar with all things
and yet brush against all in a dream.
There is only one such pair of hands in the world.

These wonderful hands of prey
I conceal under the red cloth
in defiance and melancholy, adorned with rings and strong.
These brown eyes look out in endless longing.
These red lips burn in a fire that is not quenched,
these carefree hands shall do their work in the dismally
          firelight-coloured night.

[September 1920]

My Childhood's Trees

My childhood's trees stand high in the grass
and shake their heads: what has become of you?
Rows of pillars stand like reproaches: you are unworthy to
          walk among us!
You are a child and ought to be able to do everything,
why are you fettered in the bonds of sickness?
You have become a human being, foreign and hateful.
When you were a child you conversed long with us,

182

your gaze was wise.
Now we want to tell you your life's secret:
the key to all secrets lies in the grass in the raspberry patch.
We would knock against your forehead, you sleeping one,
we would wake you, dead one, from your sleep.

[June 1922]

Churchyard Fantasy

What is it that echoes in the churchyard:
    My own! My beloved!
Who is it calling in the mist?
It is the wife of the warrior hurrying towards her husband.
An image of the Mother of God hangs on a blinding white cross
    with the child Jesus,
and the wind rocks the lilac to and fro
    over fresh graves.
And in her white bridal dress she sleeps peacefully,
    her child in her arms.
Why is your forehead so bereft of colour and pale,
    you lovely woman?
Your black locks are caressed by no one any more,
    your black locks,
and your feet in thin silk shoes,
    they feel nothing.
You fled further away than where even the sun,
    the sun shines.
You took your child in your arms and leapt,
    as swiftly as you could,
and you left behind all the stars,
    the stars beneath you.
Where the child Jesus sits at the Virgin's breast,
    there you reached
and all that a human breast can win,
    that you have won.
What is it that echoes in the churchyard:
    My own! My beloved!
Who is it calling in the mist?
It is the wife of the warrior hurrying towards her husband.

[September 1922]

O Heavenly Clarity

O heavenly clarity upon the forehead of the child –
its angel sees the Father in heaven.

And the light that streams from the eyes of the saint is as
      darkness beside
the peace that rests on the forehead of the child, the heavenly
      peace.

And the glory that shines round the brow of the saint is not
      so manifest and great
as the crown that crowns a human child of tender years.

And the fields and the flowers and the stones talk
to the child in their own language,
and the child replies to it and crows back
in the language of creation.

And God is concealed in the smallest flower
and things announce his name.
But the human heart that has been outcast by the Father
knows not how near he dwells.

[September 1922]

Homecoming

My childhood's trees stand rejoicing around me: O human!
and the grass bids me welcome from foreign lands.
I lean my head in the grass: now home at last.
Now I shall turn my back on all that lies behind me:
my only comrades shall be the forest and the shore and the lake.

Now I shall drink wisdom from the spruces' sap-filled crowns,
now I shall drink truth from the withered trunks of the birches,
now I shall drink power from the smallest and tenderest grasses:
a mighty protector mercifully reaches me his hand.

[October 1922]

184

The Moon

How all that is dead is wonderful
and ineffable:
a dead leaf and a dead human
and the moon's disc.
And all flowers know a secret
and the forest keeps it,
it is that the moon's orbit around our earth
is the path of death.
And the moon spins its wonderful web,
which the flowers love,
and the moon spins its fairy-tale net
around all that is living.
And the moon's sickle mows flowers down
on late autumn nights,
and all flowers wait for the moon's kiss
in endless longing.

[September 1922]

November Morning

The first flakes fell.
Where the waves had written their runic characters in the sand
        of the river-bed
we walked attentively. And the river-bank said to me:
Look, this is where you wandered as a child and I am still the
        same.
And the alder that stands by the water is still the same.
Say where have you wandered in foreign lands and learnt
        awkward ways?
And what have you gained? Nothing at all.

Your feet should tread this field,
here is your magic circle from the alders' catkins
certainty comes to you, and the answer to every riddle.
And you shall praise God who lets you stand in his temple
among the trees and the stones.

And you shall praise God who has let the scales fall
from your eyes.
All empty wisdom you can despise,
for now the pines and the heather are your teachers.
Bring here the false prophets, the books that lie,
we shall light in the dell by the water a merrily flaming pyre.

[October 1922]

'There is no one who has time'

There is no one who has time in the world
other than God alone.
And therefore all flowers come to Him
and the last among ants.

The forget-me-not begs Him for a higher brilliance
in its blue eyes
and the ant begs him for greater strength
with which to grasp the straw.
And the bees beg him for a mightier victory song
among the purple roses.

And God is present in every context.
When the old woman unexpectedly met her cat by the well
and the cat his housemistress.
That was a great joy for them both
but greatest of all was that God had led them together
and wished upon them this wonderful friendship
that lasted fourteen years.

And meanwhile a redstart flew out of the rowan tree by the well
happy that God had not let it fall into the hunter's claws.
But a little worm saw in a dark dream
that the moon's sickle cut his being into two parts:
the one was nothing,
the other was all things and God Himself.

186

The Land That Is Not

I long for the land that is not,
for I am weary of desiring all things that are.
The moon tells me in silver runes
about the land that is not.
The land where all our wishes are wondrously fulfilled,
the land where all our chains fall away,
the land where we cool our gashed foreheads
in the moon's dew.
My life was a hot delusion.
But I have found one thing and one thing I have truly gained –
the path to the land that is not.

In the land that is not
my beloved walks with sparkling crown.
Who is my beloved? The night is dark
and the stars tremble in answer.
Who is my beloved? What is his name?
The heavens arch higher and higher,
and a human child drowns in endless mists
and knows no answer.
But a human child is nothing other than certainty.
And it stretches out its arms higher than all heavens.
And there comes an answer: I am the one you love and always
      shall love.

Arrival in Hades

See, here is eternity's shore,
here the stream murmurs by,
and death plays in the bushes
his same monotonous melody.

Death, why were you silent?
We have come a long way
and are hungry to hear,
we have never had a nurse
who could sing like you.

The garland that never adorned my brow
I lay silently at your feet.
You shall show me a wondrous land
where the palm trees stand tall,
and where between rows of pillars
the waves of longing go.

Index of Titles and First Lines

A bird sat captured in a golden cage, 72
A Captured Bird, 72
A Counsel, 73
A few last stars glow exhaustedly, 68
A fickle moment, 87
A fiery glance has never yet betrayed, 95
Alas, that windows see, 69
A Life, 89
All my castles of air have melted like snow, 68
All people are playthings, 156
All the age's golden stars on my dark velvet dress, 102
All the Echoes in the Forest, 134
A Meeting, 85
Among grey stones, 63
And the queen asked her secret counsellor, 73
Animal Hymn, 174
An Old Ruler, 157
Approaching night, I play catch with you, 159
Are these poems? No, these are shreds, scraps, 161
Arrival in Hades, 187
A Sick Visit, 84
A Strip of Sea, 57
At last the lazybones got up, 79
At Nietzsche's Grave, 109
At Sunrise, 170
Autumn, 62
A Wish, 56

Beauty, 77
Behind the sea begin the mountains, 104
Be still, my child, nothing exists, 88
Black or White, 62
Bravery is the highest, I say to you, 123

Can you catch in your hands a star that is rising towards
    the zenith, 157
Captive, captive . . . I want to cut my fetters, 144
Captivity, 144
Christian Confession, 77

Churchyard Fantasy, 183
Creator Forms, 158
Creator's anguish round my heart, 166

Dangerous Dreams, 86
Destiny said: white you live or red you die, 75
Dionysos, 137
Do Not Gather Gold and Precious Stones, 110
Do not go too near your dreams, 86
Do not let your pride fall, 71
Dusk, 96

Early Dawn, 68
Earth, on your back I have raised a castle for conquerors, 157
Ecstasy, 171
Eros is creating the world anew, 167
Eros' Secret, 167
Eros, you cruellest of all gods, 86
Evening, 70
Evening Walk, 102
Every evening the princess let herself be caressed, 87

Farewell, 72
Far from happiness I lie on an island in the sea and sleep, 59
Fifty waggons full of hopes I had loaded to you, America,
    America, 107
First I want to climb Chimborazzo, 121
Flee into solitude! Be men, 124
Foam, 108
Foreign Lands, 70
Forest Darkness, 66
For my little songs, 84
For my own paleness' sake I love red, blue and yellow, 60
Four Little Poems, 173
Fragment, 114
Fragments of a Mood, 138
Freedom from Sorrow, 108
From 'Tales of Lilliput', 79
From the rock of destiny, 121

God, 58
God is a resting bed, on which we lie outstretched, 58

God Is Still Awake, 117
God, thou all-powerful, take pity on us, 99
Grimace d'Artiste, 99
Guard your boat from superhuman currents, 103

Hamlet, 171
Happiness has no songs, happiness has no thoughts, 81
Happiness is not what we dream of, 77
Hear the clock strike, 139
Heaven's angels sing down to earth, 163
Hell, 81
Homecoming, 184
Hope, 117
Hostile stars are rising, 158
How all that is dead is wonderful, 185
How can there be such bliss in a breast, 173
How new eyes look upon old times, 55
How shall I speak to you out of my deepest heart, 128

I, 57
I am a gypsy woman from a foreign land, 182
I am alone amidst the trees at the lake's edge, 81
I am an eagle, 175
I am a stranger in this land, 57
I am a very mature person, 174
I am beautiful, for I have grown in my beloved's garden, 84
I am blissful, 174
I am nothing but a boundless will, 145
I am no woman. I am a neuter, 59
I am the commanding strength, 157
I am the last flower of autumn, 61
I am triumphant as life itself, 173
I Believe in My Sister, 133
I bring you a single blossom-laden branch, 84
I did not find love. I met no one, 133
I do not believe in human beings, 108
I do not want to hear the mournful tale, 70
If I am a criminal, my sin cannot be measured, 111
If I Am a Liar, 111
If I do not succeed in toppling, 104
I go into the wilderness, 133
I grieve as though I had lost a fairy-tale crown, 162

I hate the thought, 113
I have a luck cat in my arms, 67
I have nothing other than my glowing cape, 99
I have powers. I fear nothing, 108
I have the net into which all fishes go, 163
I know, I know that I shall win the victory, 169
I light my light all over the Atlantic, 110
I live red. I live my blood, 167
I long for the land that is not, 187
I looked into the philosopher's house, 125
I, my own prisoner, say so, 80
In Autumn, 85
In order not to die I have to be the will to power, 170
Instinct, 168
In the Darkness, 133
In the eyes of the whole world, 131
In the Fairies' Hammock, 122
In the great forests I lost my way, 66
In the melancholy forest, 66
In the window stands a candle, 64
I once had a sister, a golden child, 134
I saw a tree that was greater than all others, 54
I saw beauty, 130
I saw that the temple of Eros was made of human bodies, 162
I sense the shadow of death, 160
I separate myself from you, 120
Is god a villain, 112
I stand as on clouds in a bliss without likeness, 162
I stand so brave, so expectant and blissful, 172
It is a strip of sea that glimmers grey, 57
It is dangerous to desire when one is the powerful one, 171
It rains, it rains on me in violent streams, 173
I turn the snakes into angels, 116
I want to be unconstrained, 117
I want to light my torches above the earth, 130
I was alone on a sunny shore, 64
I was so happy when I saw you, O sister, 90

Letters from my sister, 132
Life, 80
Life looks most like death, her sister, 78
Life sank back before me in blue smoke, 126

——life's bacteria thrive on your mucous membrane, 114
Life's champagne, 108
Life's Sister, 78
Lightning swathed in clouds, 168
Love, 74
Luck Cat, 67

Materialism, 170
Metamorphosis, 128
Might, 157
Moonlit evening, silver clear, 56
Motley Observations, 148
My artificial flowers, 122
My body is a mystery, 168
My Childhood's Trees, 182
My childhood's trees stand high in the grass, 182
My childhood's trees stand rejoicing around me, 184
My circle is narrow and the ring of my thoughts, 86
My crown is too heavy for my strength, 173
My Fairy-Tale Castles, 125
My Future, 87
My heart is kept wedged in a narrow cleft, 88
My heart is the most beautiful thing in the world, 109
My heart of iron wants to sing its song, 158
My Life, My Death and My Destiny, 145
My life was as naked, 63
My Lyre, 113
My sister, 132
My soul cannot tell stories and know any truth, 74
My soul loves foreign lands so much, 70
My soul was a light blue dress of the sky's colour, 74

Needless suffering, 65
Night and day, 122
Night is coming tall in his fleecy beard, 96
Night Madonna, 84
No bird strays here into my hidden corner, 60
Nocturne, 56
No, no, no cry all the echoes in the forest, 134
Nordic Spring, 68
Nothing, 88
November Morning, 185

Now it is autumn and the golden birds, 85
Now the earth shrouds itself once more in black, 122

O Dionysos, you come with the horses of the sun out of
    distant space, 137
Of all our sunny world, 56
O heavenly clarity upon the forehead of the child, 184
O how wonderful is hell, 81
O let me spread out my arms, life, 170
O my sunflame-coloured peaks, 100
On foot/I had to cross the solar system, 123
On the Shore, 79
On the steps of the Himalayas, 129
Orpheus, 116
Our sisters walk in motley clothes, 61
O you most glorious of all that is glorious, my body, 169
O you my heart's expanse, 170

Pain, 81
Pale-hearted night, you are listening, 144
Pale lake of autumn, 62
People,/do not gather gold and precious stones, 110
People do not know much about themselves, 127
People,/is not a storm raging across the sky, 101
People, people,/as the rain falls down from heaven, 170
People, there is a heaving in my breast, 106
Prayer, 99
Premonition, 169

Resolve, 174
Resurrection Mystery, 163
Revanche, 104
Revelation, 96
Rising stars! Teeming stars. Strange evening, 159
Roses, 141

Scherzo, 140
See, here is eternity's shore, 187
See in the sunset, 103
She sang in the dusk on the dew-wet courtyard, 75
Sick Days, 88
Sister fair, do not go up into the mountains, 73

Sister, 134
Sister, my sister, you are only little, 136
Solitude, 169
Sorrows, 73
Spring Mystery, 132,
Strange fishes glide in the depths, 69
Strange moon, 112
Strange Sea, 69
Strong Hyacinths, 97
Summer in the Mountains, 84
Sun, 174
Sunset Landscape, 103

'Tales of Lilliput', From, 79
Tantalus, Fill Your Beaker, 161
Tear down all the triumphal arches, 107
The Armoured Train, 107
The Bride, 86
The Bull, 99
The Chalice of Suffering, 124
The Charm, 128
The child of God sat with me, 135
The Colours' Longing, 60
The Complaint of the Tool, 126
The Condition, 106
The Dawn, 110
The day cools towards evening, 54
The days of autumn are translucent, 56
The Death of the Maiden, 98
The earth has been turned into an ash-heap, 125
The Elf-Queen's Sceptre, 164
The Fairy's Castle, 104
The Fields of Light, 108
The first flakes fell, 185
The first loved sweet strawberries, 77
The Footsteps of the Gods, 104
The foreign tree stands with gaudy fruits, 76
The Forest Lake, 64
The Gods Are Coming, 127
The gods go through life with their hearts high above pain, 104
The Great Garden, 175
The great hunter is dead, 109

The Gypsy Woman, 182
The Hour of Sacrifice, 139
The houses we actually live in are prehistoric huts, 148
The Hyacinth, 172
The Ineffable Is on its Way to Us, 135
The king had the word "sorrow" forbidden at court, 78
The King's Sorrow, 78
The Land That Is Not, 187
The Last Flower of Autumn, 61
The light birds high up in the air, 69
The Lightning's Yearning, 175
The little old man sits counting eggs, 98
The Lost Crown, 162
The Low Shore, 69
The Lyre of the Gods, 105
The martyr is pale, 131
The Miracle, 90
The Mirroring Well, 75
The Moon, 185
The moon knows…that blood will be shed here tonight, 102
The Moon's Secret, 102
The Most Beautiful God, 109
The Mother of God's Rose, 105
The mountains' summer is simple, 84
The Mystery, 156
The naked trees stand around your house, 62
The Net, 163
The Old House, 55
The Penitents, 124
The Planets, 159
The Portrait, 84
The Princess, 87
There are so few among the sand of the sea who understand
    it, 169
The red sun rises, 174
There is no one who has time, 186
There lies a rose in the arms of the Mother of God, 105
There once grew a tree in the forest, 98
The Ring, 131
The rivers run under the bridges, 62
The Road to Elysium and Hades, 121
The Road to Happiness, 65

The Rose, 84
The Rose Altar, 120
The Shadow of the Future, 160
The Sign, 112
The Song from off the Cloud, 102
The Song of the Ocean, 129
The Song of the Three Graves, 75
The Song of the Troubadour, 112
The Song on the Rock, 70
The Sorrowing Garden, 69
The soul of the pure maiden was never mistaken, 98
The Spirit of the Apocalypse, 106
The Star, 176
The Starry Night, 65
The Stars, 63
The stars are relentless, 89
The Statue of Beauty, 130
The Storm ('Now the earth...'), 122
The Storm ('People...'), 101
The Strong Man's Body, 169
The Sun, 162
The sun went down over the foam of the sea, 70
The Temple of Eros, 162
The Terrible Procession, 123
The Torches, 130
The Trains of the Future, 107
The Tree in the Forest, 98
The Waiting Soul, 81
The Waterfall, 166
The Whirlpool of Madness, 103
The Wood's Light Daughter, 67
The world is bathing in blood because God had to live, 101
The world is mine, 141
Thoughts about Nature, 178
Thou great Eros. Thou breathest weddings, 160
Three maidens walked hand in hand across an open plain, 85
Three Sisters, 77
To All Four Winds, 60
To a Young Woman, 95
To Eros, 86
Tolerance, 157

To the Strong, 124
Triumph of Being, 95
Two Goddesses, 71
Two Shore Poems, 63
Two Ways, 76

Uneasy Dreams, 59
Up on the clouds lives all that I need, 102
Up there stars, unambiguously clear, 140

Vierge Moderne, 59
Violet dusks I bear within me from my origins, 58

Wallenstein Profile, 159
Wandering clouds have fastened themselves to the
    mountain's edge, 64
Warm words, fine words, deep words, 65
Weaker hands may grasp the chalice of
    suffering, 124
We are all homeless wanderers, 175
We are not supposed to know, 65
We see life and death with our eyes, 178
We shall do penance in the lonely forests, 124
We women, we are so close to the brown earth, 68
What blessedness in the wind, 128
What does my mortal heart want, 171
What do you know, 176
What have i to fear? I am a part of infinity, 95
What is beauty? Ask every soul, 77
What is it that echoes in the churchyard, 183
What is my homeland, 161
What is tomorrow? Perhaps not you, 97
What is wrong with me, 118
When it rains and the sea is grey I grow sick, 79
When night comes, 63
When the black clouds marched across the sky, 85
When you saw the face of happiness you were
    disappointed, 71
Where do the gods live? In my heart, 126
Where is he, 164
Where is the bull, 99
Where is the lyre, 105

Who can love you, sister, 135
Why was life given me, 113
Wild earth that rolls onward into burning, cutting space, 159
Wilful and cold my heart has become, 72
Wind, wind, wind, 138
Without action, 106
Words, 65

You must give up your old way, 76
You who never went out of your garden plot, 57
You will not get me to believe in disgusting flies, 97

David McDuff was born in 1945. He was educated at the University of Edinburgh where he gained his Ph.D in 1971 with a thesis on the poetry of the Russian modernist Innokenty Annensky, having spent several periods of study in the Soviet Union. After some years of foreign travel and freelance writing, he worked as a co-editor of the literary quarterly *Stand*, and also with Anvil Press Poetry in London.

He is currently working on new translations of the novels of Dostoyevsky for the Penguin Classics series; his translations of Dostoyevsky's *The House of the Dead* and *Poor Folk and other Stories* have appeared in the Classics, along with Tolstoy's *The Kreutzer Sonata* and *The Sebastopol Sketches*, and a volume of Leskov – *Lady Macbeth of Mtsensk* and other stories. Dostoyevsky's *Crime and Punishment* and a new volume of Dostoyevsky stories, *Uncle's Dream*, are forthcoming.

David McDuff's poetry translations include *Osip Mandelstam: Selected Poems*, published by Farrar, Straus & Giroux in 1975 (and now available in paperback from Anvil Press); Edith Södergran's *Complete Poems* (Bloodaxe Books, 1984); *No, I'm Not Afraid* by Irina Ratushinskaya (Bloodaxe Books, 1986); the *Selected Poems* of Marina Tsvetayeva (Bloodaxe Books, 1987) and *Ice Around Our Lips: Finland-Swedish Poetry* (Bloodaxe Books, 1989).

He has translated many poets, essayists and novelists – Russian, Austrian, Swedish, Norwegian, Icelandic and Lithuanian – including Joseph Brodsky, Anna Akhmatova, Vasily Rozanov, Robert Musil, Gunnar Ekelöf, Ólafur Gunnarsson and Tomas Venclova.

His first collection of poems, *Words in Nature*, was published by the Ramsay Head Press in Edinburgh in 1972. He now lives in Greenwich, London.

Lightning Source UK Ltd.
Milton Keynes UK
UKHW010731270722
406409UK00001B/133